ReEnvisioning the Material Past

AF291295

Glenda Swan

ReEnvisioning the Material Past

How to Educate and Engage Modern Students Using Visual Culture

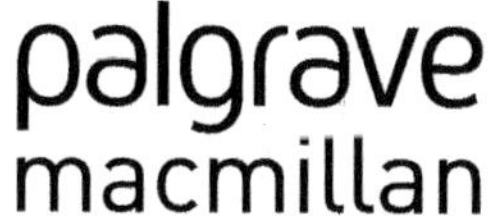

Glenda Swan
Valdosta State University
Valdosta, GA, USA

ISBN 978-3-031-24026-3   ISBN 978-3-031-24027-0   (eBook)
https://doi.org/10.1007/978-3-031-24027-0

© The Editor(s) (if applicable) and The Author(s), under exclusive licence to Springer Nature Switzerland AG 2023
This work is subject to copyright. All rights are solely and exclusively licensed by the Publisher, whether the whole or part of the material is concerned, specifically the rights of translation, reprinting, reuse of illustrations, recitation, broadcasting, reproduction on microfilms or in any other physical way, and transmission or information storage and retrieval, electronic adaptation, computer software, or by similar or dissimilar methodology now known or hereafter developed.
The use of general descriptive names, registered names, trademarks, service marks, etc. in this publication does not imply, even in the absence of a specific statement, that such names are exempt from the relevant protective laws and regulations and therefore free for general use.
The publisher, the authors, and the editors are safe to assume that the advice and information in this book are believed to be true and accurate at the date of publication. Neither the publisher nor the authors or the editors give a warranty, expressed or implied, with respect to the material contained herein or for any errors or omissions that may have been made. The publisher remains neutral with regard to jurisdictional claims in published maps and institutional affiliations.

This Palgrave Macmillan imprint is published by the registered company Springer Nature Switzerland AG.
The registered company address is: Gewerbestrasse 11, 6330 Cham, Switzerland

Abstract

While images are omnipresent and influential in contemporary culture, they are rarely subjected to analysis, which is why "Representation" needs to be added to the "Three R's" of essential educational skills. Making visual literacy a core component in higher education, though, means that students will need to develop this skill across the curriculum, even when the subject does not directly address modern digital culture. This book is designed to help instructors effectively incorporate images and other aspects of material culture into their pedagogy in an engaging and relatable manner. The author draws on her personal experiences as an historian of ancient art who instructs a wide variety of undergraduates. In addition to helping students look and think critically, the book will explore how the material culture of the past can be a potent tool in motivating student involvement with course content and sharpening skills vital for navigating contemporary culture.

CONTENTS

CHAPTER 1

Introduction

In today's contemporary world, images are with us all the time, as electronic devices have become an omnipresent accessory. The images that fill these devices not only are used to inform, persuade, and sell, but also play a significant role in the communications between people within social media.[1] Yet, despite the ubiquity and influence of images in modern life, visual literacy has still not been systematically incorporated as a foundational aspect of higher education.[2] Often educators mistakenly assume that since students have grown up in this image-rich environment they already know how to evaluate and produce effective images.[3] Moreover, even within the field of educational research, the use of visual analysis remains underutilized and understudied.[4]

While people's interactions with images may often be powerful, they are also typically very brief. Even within a museum setting—where one presumes people come to look—studies have shown that paintings only receive around 17 seconds of attention from a viewer.[5] Technology continues to reinforce this practice, with applications like SnapChat or Instagram Stories that set short amounts of time for the process of viewing, as well as with hardware that makes image consumption even faster and more compelling.[6] So, it is important that students become accustomed to looking longer at images, as analysis requires this investment of time. However, it is equally important that instructors strive to make sure that this investment of time is rewarded.

There are many ways that images can be subjected to visual analysis, both in terms of the larger theoretical approach[7] and how that approach is translated

---

[1] Hand (2017).
[2] Kędra (2018).
[3] Judd (2018).
[4] Schreiber and Fischman (2017).
[5] Smith and Smith (2001).
[6] Rolo et al. (2020).
[7] Ledin and Machin (2018).

© The Author(s), under exclusive license to Springer Nature Switzerland AG 2023

G. Swan, *ReEnvisioning the Material Past*,
https://doi.org/10.1007/978-3-031-24027-0_1

1

into pedagogical practices.[8] While use of some of the basic terminology of elements and principles of design has shown to aid visual analysis,[9] the process does not require specific vocabulary. It is critical, though, that the viewer consider not simply the image itself, but the context of that image—not only at the time it was created, but also in its later reception. Fortunately, in the age of memes and fanfiction, this is not actually a foreign concept for students, even if they will need help to becoming accustomed to applying it to less familiar material. Indeed, the digital culture in which students regularly interact and communicate allows for rich new relationships with visual culture.[10]

Still, the challenges associated with the academic study of images appear compounded when one is teaching in a subject area that does not appear to have any natural connections with contemporary culture or media. I have found, however, that by changing the ways in which students interact with materials from the past, they are more likely to be engaged critical thinkers. Indeed, the content's distance from the present can even prove somewhat liberating for students, as it can appear at first to be a welcome change from the world of social media that demands so much of their attention. While subsequent chapters of the book will share some of the specific approaches and methods that have proved successful in my classroom, I wanted to spend the rest of this introduction explaining the experiences that have influenced my approach to teaching.

The inception of this book came out of my own frustration in encountering interesting pedagogical concepts and practices that I knew I would probably never be able to employ. Over the course of my career, there have been a great many reasons why I never adopted a single, regular teaching methodology into my pedagogy, but most have been centered around the nature of my position, students, load, class size, room layout, resources, and type of institution. Even though I study art within the context of its creation and reception within Greco-Roman culture as an ancient art historian and archeologist, it took me time to realize that truly effective pedagogy also needed to be situated to its context. I now realize that my career has forged me into a multi-tool, and there have been many times when that adaptability has been a real lifesaver, both for myself and for my students. Indeed, my belief in "survivalist" teaching—by which I mean applicable and achievable pedagogical strategies to be employed as needed—was only strengthened by the disruption that COVID brought. Although I will be focused only on my own experiences, I suspect that aspects of my experience will resonate with all those who find themselves teaching "in the trenches" of academia rather than in the oft imagined "ivory tower."

When I was first starting my academic career, I was just finishing grad school at an ivy league school and was completely unaware that scholarship on pedagogy even existed. Even if I had known, though, I was much too busy

---

[8] Beatty (2013).
[9] Williams (2019).
[10] Favero (2014).

preparing new courses in subjects I had never even studied before, as my graduate training focused on the material culture of ancient Greece and Rome as contextualized within the study of classical languages and literature. While most academic positions in ancient art had been based in these types of departments in the past, these types of positions were already on the decline even before I earned by PhD. As a result, my first teaching position was as the only art historian in a studio arts department; I had a 4-4 load and taught around 250 art majors and general educations students a semester with no type of teaching assistance.

I will credit most of my success in this challenging endeavor to the fact that I was a good researcher and very determined to be a good teacher. I found useful sources, prepared presentations, and was always ready in time for each class meeting; while I certainly made mistakes, I worked hard to learn from failure as well as success. Soon, though, I had something of a revelation: most of my students didn't know how to be effective students in my courses. Moreover, the students who seemed to be having the most difficulty were the first- and second-year students in my general education courses, which I within a large auditorium. While these most non-major students appeared to be the subject of little attention or interest by administration, those courses represented the majority of my teaching in terms of the number of students involved.

The quest to learn more about effective teaching finally led me to discover the Scholarship of Teaching and Learning (SoTL). While this really expanded my perspective into pedagogy, most of the studies were in fields very different from my own and often involved more specialized courses with fewer students, so these pedagogical approaches often required creative adaptation for use in my own course, if they could be employed at all. Even though I suspect I often learned more from the "error" portion of trial and error, I was discovering much more about how my students learned along with my own outlook and methods as a teacher. I began to get interested in sharing some on my own successes within SoTL conferences publications. Unfortunately, I soon discovered that articles about pedagogy would not be considered as evidence of my academic research at the new position I had recently accepted at a private liberal arts college. While most of my courses were now in ancient art history, I was still required to teach some large general education courses. However, these courses were very different than any I had ever experienced as either a student or an instructor, as they were collaborative courses for all first-year students that involved several different disciplines. In contrast to many instructors around campus, I found teaching these courses to be very interesting, despite many of the inherent challenges that came along with them.

It was in these collaborative multidisciplinary courses that I focused most strongly on making my own visual culture content more engaging and approachable, both for the presentation of that content within our large group lectures and for our smaller individual discussion sections. Although my most significant contributions were focused on ancient art and archeology, I still worked to make examples of material culture applicable to all the other required course content and happily shared my examples with other instructors in the course. I also employed these materials to meet the overarching goal of the course itself, which was to reflect on the larger societal questions that humanity not only has faced in the past, but also continues to struggle with to this day. So, when discussion of the course material from the past raised a question about some other socio-culture issue—even if it was from another place or time from the course material that was the topic for discussion that day—these questions still seemed very appropriate to the objectives of the course. In practice, though, this meant I was fielding questions about art, literature, and culture from a variety of times and places. At first, I was somewhat embarrassed to admit when I did not know about something, although I always made sure to come back the next class meeting with more informed reflections on the questions that had stumped me. Still, it was quickly evident that this practice was activating student learning and, by actively modeling the process of academic inquiry, I found I was simply altering my role as instructor rather than diminishing it.

Regrettably, though, I began to realize that my approach to making my ancient art content more accessible and relevant was received differently by my departmental colleagues, who recommended that I treat the discipline of art history with more authority and seriousness. This perspective of presenting myself as "the sage on the stage,"[11] where I would demonstrate to my students how erudite I was and present them with knowledge to learn, reminded me of my graduate training, where I was told that in order to be seen as an expert in my field, any questions about my work while presenting at an academic conference should be viewed as a challenge and should be responded to accordingly. However, my lived experience was telling me that people who went to the conferences that I was attending appeared friendly and interested in what I and others had to share. I know I personally saw these meetings as a wonderful way to hear about what scholars were doing in my field, particularly as my engagement with my research had altered dramatically since graduate school, where I had easy access to well-stocked research libraries and colleagues in my exact field with which to confer. Besides, wasn't the point of education—at every level—supposed to be about learning?

A period of personal reflection followed that eventually led to me accepting another position. I was now teaching at a much less prestigious institution and had returned to a 4-4 teaching load as the only art historian in a studio arts department along with larger general education courses related to the arts. Fortunately, though, I found appreciation from faculty as well as students for my pedagogy, even though I was regularly using many techniques—problem-solving, role-playing, making connections to modern media culture, and the like—that certainly would have indicated a real lack of seriousness to some colleagues within my discipline. In this new position, I was even asked to create and teach an online Art Appreciation course. While I learned a little bit about

---

[11] King (1993).

learning management systems and other technologies, I soon realized that these programs were simply tools—even if they happened to be new ones to me—and it was the application of these electronic tools that was crucially important. This experience led me to reflect on the ways in which students learn in a yet another new context. While online learning was certainly different than face-to-face learning, I came to realize that it was not as different as I had first imagined.

Larger issues ultimately led me to accept a position at a regional comprehensive institution as one of the two art historians in a studio arts department. While my load was still 4-4, class sizes were smaller and I could focus more on the ancient art that was my academic specialty; for example, while I still taught Art History Survey, I only taught the first half that studied art up to the time of the Renaissance. I also had the opportunity to teach some upper-division topic courses of my own choosing to studio art majors, even though the focus was on helping the students to learn how to write and research more than amassing detailed knowledge of the ancient world. My discussion about how I adapted these courses into active learning course that involved student research is the subject of a later chapter. I also taught some general education courses, such as Introduction to Visual Arts, but I was able to develop a new general education course of my own design focused on the depiction of myth in material culture from around the world; unlike most mythology course and their accompanying texts, I put the emphasis on the images as well as the contextualization on these images, although I did employ both primary and secondary source support.

Student responses to all my courses has been overwhelmingly positive even though there is no major in art history. Indeed, so many contemporary studio art majors made requests for my upper-division topic courses in ancient art history that I now teach one every semester. This student interest has motivated the proposal of a minor in art history, which is currently passing through the process of curricular review. I attribute the success of these courses to how the ancient material has been made assessable and relatable to non-specialists. Still, I believe that images of material culture do not need to be the focus of an entire course; instructors from every discipline can interject a little visual analysis into their course to add another aspect of analysis and engagement to their own engagement with the course material. It is also helpful to ask students to do the same in connection with their own research. Visual communication is something that I have helped to incorporate as part of my university's Undergraduate Research Council, which holds a yearly undergraduate research symposium; there are awards not only for best papers, but also for best posters submissions and three-minute videos.

This book is designed to help instructors reimagine how they might actively involve their students with visual analysis and communication in ways that contemporary, career-minded students will perceive as interesting and potentially useful, even when the subject matter is not from contemporary media culture. In keeping with this goal, the style of writing in this monograph is intended to be similarly approachable and relatable. While the methods and techniques discussed here are supported by many years of experience and research—along with specific examples that I use in my own courses—my goal is not to be authoritative or proscriptive. I would encourage instructors to try whatever variety of methods they feel might have the best chance of helping their students succeed, not simply in the content of their courses, but as critical viewers in a world filled with screens.

The following chapters will outline some effective approaches for: incorporating visual analysis into courses, making the past more engaging to modern students, discovering ways that students can engage actively with the materials of the past, and designing activities that allow students to make their own connections with material culture and then sharing those discoveries with their peers.

REFERENCES

Beatty, Nicole A. "Cognitive Visual Literacy: From Theories and Competencies to Pedagogy." *Art Documentation: Journal of the Art Libraries Society of North America* 32, no. 1 (2013): 33–42.

Favero, Paolo. "Learning to Look Beyond the Frame: Reflections on the Changing Meaning of Images in the Age of Digital Media Practices." *Visual Studies* 29, no. 2 (2014): 166–179.

Hand, Martin. "Visuality in Social Media: Researching Images, Circulations and Practices." In *The SAGE Handbook of Social Media Research Methods*, edited by Luke Sloan and Anabel Quan-Haase, 217–231 (Thousand Oaks, CA: SAGE Publishing, 2017).

Judd, Terry. "The Rise and Fall (?) of the Digital Natives." *Australasian Journal of Educational Technology* 34, no. 5 (2018): 99–119.

Kędra, Joanna. "What Does It Mean to Be Visually Literate? Examination of Visual Literacy Definitions in a Context of Higher Education." *Journal of Visual Literacy* 37, no. 2 (2018): 67–84.

King, Alison. "From Sage on the Stage to Guide on the Side." *College Teaching* 41, no. 1 (1993): 30–35.

Ledin, Per, and David Machin. *Doing Visual Analysis: From Theory to Practice* (London: Sage Publications, 2018).

Rolo, Ema, Helena Nobre, and Vania Baldi. "Screens Affordances in Image Consumption." In Vol. 2, *Proceedings of the Future Technologies Conference (FTC) 2019*, Volume 2, edited by Kohei Arai, Rahul Bhatia, Supriya Kapoor, 176–187 (Cham, Switzerland: Springer, 2020).

Schreiber, Constantin, and Gustavo E. Fischman. "The Visual Turn in Comparative and International Education Research." In *Handbook on Comparative and International Studies in Education*, edited by Donald K. Sharpes, 127–152 (Charlotte, NC: Information Age Publishing, Inc., 2017).

Smith, Jeffrey K., and Lisa F. Smith. "Spending Time on Art." *Empirical Studies of the Arts* 19, no. 2 (2001): 229–236.

Williams, Wendy R. "Attending to the Visual Aspects of Visual Storytelling: Using Art and Design Concepts to Interpret and Compose Narratives with Images." *Journal of Visual Literacy* 38, no. 1–2 (2019): 66–82.

CHAPTER 2

Taking the Time to Look, Learning the Skills to See

Today's students, we have been told, are digital natives.[1] Considering the number of devices that students bring into the classroom, it certainly seems difficult to argue with this idea. However, the real issue is not what new technologies our students now consider essential to their daily existence, but how we can get students to look more critically at whatever is being presented to them on those screens, now as well as in the future.[2] Teaching them to analyze what they see along with the context in which it is presented is critical to creating cognizant and discerning viewers. However, students will need to learn these skills not simply passively as viewers, but also actively as effective presenters of images. Understanding how to effectively employ images themselves will also help to make them more effective multimodal communicators, which is increasingly becoming an expectation for twenty-first-century employment.[3]

It is critical that "Representations" be added to the "Three R's" of essential educational skills. Still, while the need for building visual literary skills among

---

[1] A review of the issues associated with the notion of "digital natives" can be found in Chris Evans and Wenqian Robertson, "The Four Phases of the Digital Natives Debate," *Human Behavior and Emerging Technologies* 2, no. 3 (2020): 269–277.

[2] Digital competency is not simply achieved with more screen time. See Konstantina Martzoukou, Crystal Fulton, Petros Kostagiolas, and Charilaos Lavranos, "A Study of Higher Education Students' Self-perceived Digital Competences for Learning and Everyday Life Online Participation," *Journal of Documentation* 76, no. 6 (2020): 1413–1458, which discusses how an academic approach to digital information involves different skills and approaches than a familiarity with social media and online consumerism.

[3] Even if employers do not typically use the term multimodal, the different communication skills they seek do align with that definition; see Tina A. Coffelt, Dale Grauman, and Frances L. M. Smith, "Employers' Perspectives on Workplace Communication Skills: The Meaning of Communication Skills," *Business and Professional Communication Quarterly* 82, no. 4 (2019): 418–439.

© The Author(s), under exclusive license to Springer Nature Switzerland AG 2023
G. Swan, *ReEnvisioning the Material Past,*
https://doi.org/10.1007/978-3-031-24027-0_2

undergraduates has been the subject of discussion for over a decade,[4] there has been no clear agreement on the definition of visual literacy or the most effective approach for incorporating into the curriculum. While courses in art history have been shown to be a natural and effective for teaching such skills,[5] most institutions of higher education do not require students to take courses within that specific discipline as part of their general education curriculum.[6] Nevertheless, for students to truly master all the skills required for visual literacy, it is important for educators in every discipline to help model, instruct, and assess visual communication within their classroom, even if the focus in the classroom is not on either images or contemporary culture. Indeed, not only seeing these skills employed within different contexts reflects the variety of content and contexts of images within contemporary culture, but the latter's presence across the curriculum will help to establish it as a core competency among students.

There are many other potential benefits for faculty interested in helping students to establish these skills. Because images are such an integral part of their daily lives, most students find images—even when in association with some text or numerical data—more approachable and engaging.[7] Therefore, images can help students feel more connected to the material, which can be particularly important when the subject being discussed does not seem immediately relevant to their contemporary lives or future profession.[8] Nevertheless, one of the first lessons that students need to be taught is that images deserve time, attention, and study,[9] as most people have become habituated in responding to images in a superficial or emotional manner, despite being aware that digital images can be easily manipulated.[10]

[4] For a bibliographic review, see Dana Statton Thompson, "Recommended Reads for Visual Literacy: An Online Bibliography of Articles, Books, and Archival Materials," *Art Documentation: Journal of the Art Libraries Society of North America* 39, no. 2 (2020): 239–246.

[5] Sarah Archino, "Addressing Visual Literacy in the Survey: Balancing Transdisciplinary Competencies and Course Content," *Art History Pedagogy & Practice* 5, no. 1 (2020): 1–14.

[6] Kevin D. Gwaltney, "General Education Requirements: A Look at the Structure of Higher Education" (Prepared for the Missouri General Assembly Joint Committee on Education on August 19, 2020), http://www.senate.mo.gov/jced/GeneralEducationRequirementsRethinking theStructureofHigherEducation.pdf.

[7] David Roberts, "The Engagement Agenda, Multimedia Learning and the Use of Images in Higher Education Lecturing: or, How to End Death by PowerPoint," *Journal of Further and Higher Education* 42, no. 7 (2018): 969–985.

[8] This can also apply to instruction in the course content itself, as demonstrated in a study by Jerrod H. Yarosh, "The Syllabus Reconstructed: An Analysis of Traditional and Visual Syllabi for Information Retention and Inclusiveness," *Teaching Sociology* 49, no. 2 (2021): 173–183.

[9] I make this an introductory focus on even in courses where the art historical analysis of images is a focus; see Glenda Swan, "Building a Foundation for Survey: Employing a Focused Introduction," *Art History Pedagogy & Practice* (2016): 1–18, https://academicworks.cuny.edu/cgi/viewcontent.cgi?article=1001&context=ahpp.

[10] Allison J. Lazard, Mary A. Bock, and Michael S. Mackert, "Impact of Photo Manipulation and Visual Literacy on Consumers' Responses to Persuasive Communication," *Journal of Visual Literacy* 39, no. 2 (2020): 90–110.

The first step for the instructor is to look with a critical eye at the images that are employed within the classroom. The instructor can be an effective model for students, so how the instructor employs and discusses images in a course can be both directly and indirectly influential on students.[11] Therefore, it is important to make sure images are being integrated into class discussion rather than simply being objects of unremarked display, which is their most common role.[12] For example, rather than using an image next to text, consider making the image the focus of the slide. Limiting text not only helps with students' mental processing of the content in the PowerPoint, but also allows students to comprehend contemporaneous discussion more effectively.[13] Consider using abbreviated PowerPoints within classroom and then posting PowerPoints to highlight important points about the content on an online learning management system after class.[14] There are many ways that an instructor can use a slide with a single image in class:

- Before the start of a topic to generate student interest as well as get a measure of existing student knowledge;
- during the discussion of a topic to ask students to apply points that have recently been made;
- periodically throughout the discussion of a topic to generate alternate approaches and perspectives, which also reminds students about the diversity of experiences and viewpoints that exist in regard to a topic; or
- after the conclusion of a topic for review and reinforcement.

Using PowerPoints in this way also places greater emphasis on the importance of the active engagements with course content that happen within the classroom, thereby helping to motivate attendance and, most importantly,

---

[11] The professor's mindset and approach in class does impact students, as seen in the study by Katherine Muenks et al., "Does My Professor Think My Ability Can Change? Students' Perceptions of Their STEM Professors' Mindset Beliefs Predict Their Psychological Vulnerability, Engagement, and Performance in Class," *Journal of Experimental Psychology: General* 149, no. 11 (2020): 2119–2144.

[12] Refer to the study by Madeline J. Hallewell and Natasa Lackovic, "Do Pictures 'Tell' a Thousand Words in Lectures? How Lecturers Vocalise Photographs in Their Presentations," *Higher Education Research & Development* 36, no. 6 (2017): 1166–1180.

[13] A review of the literature on PowerPoint usage as well as the many variables that impact its effectiveness can be found in David Chávez Herting, Ramón Cladellas Pros, and Antoni Castelló Tarrida, "Patterns of PowerPoint Use in Higher Education: A Comparison Between the Natural, Medical, and Social Sciences," *Innovative Higher Education* 45, no. 1 (2020): 65–80.

[14] Surprisingly, I found that access to these resources did not impact student attendance, which has also been supported in a study by Naomi K. Grant and April L. McGrath, "Effects of PowerPoint Slides on Attendance and Learning: If You Share It, They Will (Still) Come," *Scholarship of Teaching and Learning in Psychology* (2021): 1–7, https://doi.org/10.1037/stl0000241. While providing PowerPoints to students has not shown demonstrable impact on student learning, there are many variables that could be influencing these results, such as when the PowerPoints are made available to students and the extensiveness of the written material provided within them.

participation.[15] Additionally, class discussion is useful for the promotion of diverse perspectives into course content because it allows students to hear different interpretations of the same image directly from others; this is particularly helpful for dismantling the idea that images communicate some single, universal message.[16] I design my classroom PowerPoints with the plan of having students make the points that I otherwise would have presented myself; of course, I also plan to direct the discussion as needed with directed prompts. This approach not only helps with time management, but also serves to forefront the importance of both visual content and student contributions within my classroom; I save even more time by preparing the more elaborated PowerPoint for posting first and then editing it to create the version that I will present in class.

There are a lot of effective methods for choosing images for presentation in a PowerPoint. One useful approach is to select an image that contains some visual element that provides larger insight into a cultural belief or practice from a particular time or place that has already been the object of some class discussion. For example, many African cultural values clearly manifest themselves in its art. Before I start displaying African art, however, I will ask students to associate concepts like intelligence, power, and spirituality with a part of their own body; most students will respectively point to their head, hand, and heart. With this preparation, students are typically quick to associate the exaggerated size of the head with a form of cultural expression rather than a lack of artistic skill in the depiction of proportions. This type of larger instructional goal allows me to choose from many different figurative works from Africa that would be appropriate for this discussion.

Sometimes it can be effective to focus on contextualizing an image depicted in a PowerPoint. Then, one can explain to students how it was misinterpreted outside of its original cultural context and/or removed by outsiders without concern for what it meant to the people who made and used it. Unfortunately, history is rich many examples of how non-Christian objects of religious power were referred to as fetishes or idols and then collected as souvenirs;[17] also consider discussing the ways in which ancient material culture—which sometimes even included human remains—was presented to the public by museums.[18] Of

---

[15] The significance of student engagement rather than simple attendance even in this age of online learning has been made by Stefan Büchele, "Evaluating the Link Between Attendance and Performance in Higher Education: The Role of Classroom Engagement Dimensions," *Assessment & Evaluation in Higher Education* 46, no. 1 (2021): 132–150.

[16] For an example students can relate to, consult the discussion regarding common misinterpretations of emoji in Qiyu Bai et al., "A Systematic Review of Emoji: Current Research and Future Perspectives," *Frontiers in Psychology* 10 (2019): 1–16, https://www.frontiersin.org/articles/10.3389/fpsyg.2019.02221/full.

[17] To view an easily accessible example, see Victoria Hobbs, "The Function of a 'Fetish' Figure," *V&A Conservation Journal 31* (1999), http://www.vam.ac.uk/content/journals/conservation-journal/issue-31/the-function-of-a-fetish-figure/.

[18] The scholarship on the role museums in promoting bias is extensive, but change is actively being sought by many museum professionals, minority groups, and even artists; aspects of all these issues are addressed in Jenny Kidd et al., ed., *Challenging History in the Museum: International Perspectives* (London: Routledge, 2016).

course, images can also be employed to offer a counterpoint perspective to a dominate narrative. For example, while ancient texts appear to assert that women's labor in fifth-century Athens was—as well as should be—restricted to the home, there are some images on pottery that depict women laboring outside of the home.[19] This example is a useful reminder that the people of the past were not homogeneous, and that the literacy of the elite classes made them the most common authors and audience for ancient texts.

Often, though, it can be surprisingly impactful to simply to select a well-known object for display in a PowerPoint. Not only is it easier to find accessible academic discussion on often-reproduced images, but there is also a better chance it may seem more accessible to students. As I will discuss in more detail in a moment, discovering unexpected information in famous works can be particularly impactful because students tend to overestimate their understanding of well-known images. Ultimately, though, I hope this discussion has made clear that there are many images that make good choices for presentation to students, so don't be concerned about selecting a "wrong" image. Indeed, if there are images that you already know a little bit about and find interesting or exciting, those are the best choice, as this type of sharing with been shown to make both the instructor and the material seem more relatable to many students.[20]

Below is a summary of some useful aspects to reflect on when selecting an image for presentation:

- The image relates effectively to an objective associated with the content of that lesson.
- The image has at least one accessible visual element that reflects an aspect of its period and/or culture under discussion.
- The image helps to provide more tangible insight into something more conceptual under discussion.
- The complexity of the image is either appropriate to the time allotted for discussion or the discussion of a complex image will be limited in its focus.
- The history of the collection, display, or academic discussion of the image is useful for providing more insight into how the original context of the image was not correctly considered.
- It is easy to secure a good quality image for display as well as access clear and effective academic discussion about that image.
- The image is one in which you have knowledge or interest.

---

[19] For both textual and visual evidence, see Marjorie Susan Venit, "The Caputi Hydria and Working Women in Classical Athens" *The Classical World* 81, no. 4 (1988): 265–272.

[20] Amy Chasteen Miller and Brooklyn Mills, "'If They Don't Care, I Don't Care': Millennial and Generation Z Students and the Impact of Faculty Caring," *Journal of the Scholarship of Teaching and Learning* 19, no. 4 (2019): 78–89.

It is important to take some time with images in class in order to model good visual analysis practices for students and draw attention to the fact that most people treat images in a very quick and cursory manner. Indeed, even with many famous images that students think they know, I have found that students have rarely reflected upon or even looked at very closely at them; so, teaching students something new about a familiar image can be a good way to create an impact about the importance of close looking. For example, people often describe the clocks in Dali's famous *Persistence of Memory* painting as "melting," but is this really the best word to describe them?[21] This type of query is also useful for asking students to think carefully about how specific words convey meaning, as well as how they can use visual observations from within a work as evidence to support or refute an argument. Usually, students will slowly marshal points against such a characterization, noting how the depiction of light in the work does not feel strong enough for melting and how the insects suggest something more akin to deterioration and decay. Another approach is to provide students with an image and ask them to describe it to another student who cannot see it; while this activity does take some time, it really helps students to appreciate both close looking and effective description.

Analyzing photographs is a particularly effective way to make the point that visual evidence does not speak for itself. Students have become very accustomed to seeing photos in many contexts without little to no analysis of the image, the photographer, or the original context of the photo. Even though Duane Michals' photograph "This Is My Proof" is from 1967, it is an example that is very relatable to modern students because of the commonality of photographs within social media. The work depicts a clothed man and a woman sitting on bed while the woman hugs the man's back; a handwritten text below that image reads: "This photograph is my proof. There was that afternoon, when things were still good between us, and she embraced me, and we were so happy. It did happen, she did love me. Look see for yourself!"[22] Students will typically start by taking about how the photo feels persuasive, but then the discussion will tend to reverse itself and students will end up questioning the validity of the image; they will note how the figures look posed, the setting looks staged, and the language of the text makes it seem as though it is trying too hard to be convincing, all of which ultimately makes the claim of authenticity seem less well-founded.

While Duane Michals was indeed manufacturing narratives within his photo, it is important to have students recognize how the tension between reality and construction is inherent to the photographic medium. This dichotomy can also be effectively explored using photographs that are often employed in

---

[21] An image and discussion of the work—excerpted from *MoMA Highlights: 375 Works from The Museum of Modern Art, New York* (New York: The Museum of Modern Art, 2019)—posted on the museum's website at https://www.moma.org/collection/works/79018.

[22] A detailed analysis of the work can be found in Teresa Winterhalter, "Desire Under the Lens: Critical Perspective in a Duane Michals Photograph," *Literature and Theology* 11, no. 3 (1997): 229–238.

connection with historical studies, most of which students are already familiar with from textbooks. Even just a quick investigation into many of the most famous "documentary" photographs of the historical past—such as the American Civil War, nineteenth-century images of the American West, the Dust Bowl, early twentieth-century New York tenements, or the Harlem Renaissance—provides important insights into the construction of these images. At times, the construction of these images could even be quite literal, as in the Civil War photographer Alexander Gardner, who posed bodies after death to create more compelling narratives in both visual and textual formats.[23] Nevertheless, it is always important to reflect on how a photograph was selected, composed, lit, and presented, as well as how all that framing contributes viewers' experience of the photo and, ultimately, their understanding of its subject.[24] The pervasiveness of images in every aspect of contemporary media make this not simply an issue in regard to images of the past.[25] Showing how visual images need the same degree of analysis as textual and numerical evidence will help students to be more effective members of modern society as well as scholars.[26]

In order to make the case to students that close looking and visual analysis is a useful skill in today's visual world, it is helpful to demonstrate how much unwitting consumption of images there is in our modern visual culture. Student knowledge of advertising is extensive, so artworks that appropriate imagery from such sources are an excellent way for students to appreciate the persuasive power of images. I like to show Heidi Cody's 2000 work *American Alphabet*, which depicts the alphabet using individual letters from different product brands, because students will immediately start announcing the source of each letter, such as the O from Oreo cookies.[27] However, I like to wait until the class starts to struggle with some of the letters for products that are no longer being produced and then ask them why they are bothered by the fact that they didn't recognize a handful of products rather than being disturbed by how easily they

<hr>

[23] See "The Case of the Moved Body," Library of Congress, https://www.loc.gov/collections/civil-war-glass-negatives/articles-and-essays/does-the-camera-ever-lie/the-case-of-the-moved-body/.

[24] A helpful approach to understanding how these images reflect constructed knowledge rather than unmeditated truth can be found in Christopher Carter, *Rhetorical Exposures: Confrontation and Contradiction in US Social Documentary Photography* (Tuscaloosa: The University of Alabama Press, 2015).

[25] For a recent book that focuses on documentary images in contemporary culture, see Michelle Bogre, *Documentary Photography Reconsidered: History, Theory and Practice* (New York: Routledge, 2020).

[26] A useful resource for those interested in how they might find and employ images in their own research is Gillian Rose, *Visual Methodologies: An Introduction to Researching with Visual Materials*, 4th ed. (London: Sage, 2016).

[27] More information about the work and how it can be used in the classroom can be found in Kevin Tavin, "Heidi Cody: Letters to the World and the ABCs of Visual Culture," in *Culture as Commons: Art and Social Justice Education*, eds. Therese M. Quinn, John Ploof and Lisa J. Hochtritt (New York: Routledge, 2012), 9–10.

did recognize most of these products from only a single letter. I then like to follow this up with a discussion of Shepard Fairey's *Obey* project, which started in 1989, and involved placing stickers with no clear message in public places; although Fairey discussed the work as an demonstration of how viewers became frustrated by the appearance of stickers in public spaces because they were not used to looking at images where the product or motive is not obvious,[28] the artist has since adapted that image into a contemporary commercial production brand.[29] Of course, the fact that advertisers have not only used similar forms of guerrilla marketing, but even worked with graffiti artists to promote products is yet another example of how much depth and complexity can come from the consideration of all the context(s) in which an image may appear.[30]

Outside of the classroom, though, be sure to take a close look at the images that are included in assigned textbook or readings and make them as part of the analysis as well. This is a task that can also be rewarding for students to do on their own. Activities can ask students to consider what images were selected for the text or article and how they present information in conjunction with as well as in comparison to the text. Keep in mind that this type of visual analysis does not have to be restricted to images and can also include any method where information is conveyed visually, such as an infographic, chart, or graph; indeed, close looking paired with an analysis of the visual choices made is the beginning of basic visual analysis and can certainly be applied to the visual presentation of data.[31] The next step is to ask students to reflect on not only what material is selected for presentation, but also how that material is being presented. The manner of presentation is critical for understanding what an image is expected to evoke from viewers, as it is being employed within a specific context; prompting students to consider if they can think of any parallels with how they have seen imagery employed in modern media can be very useful for this type of approach, as it can make the context more relatable.[32]

Still, it is important to keep in mind that most viewers still consider images to be illustrative, which can make them very passively persuasive.[33] For this reason, it can be very helpful to have students reflect on how images use their

---

[28] Shepard Fairey, "Manifesto," 1990, https://obeygiant.com/.

[29] "Obey," Obey Clothing, 2023, https://obeyclothing.com/.

[30] A good source for further reading on this topic is Damien Droney, "The Business of "Getting Up": Street Art and Marketing in Los Angeles," *Visual Anthropology* 23, no. 2 (2010): 98–114.

[31] A useful discussion regarding the impact of design choices associated with the presentation of visual data can be found in Danielle Albers Szafir, "The Good, the Bad, and the Biased: Five Ways Visualizations Can Mislead (and How to Fix Them)," *Interactions* 25, no. 4 (2018): 26–33.

[32] For a method of analyzing visual images employed in contemporary media culture based on semiotics, see Natasa Lackovic, "Thinking with Digital Images in the Post-Truth Era: A Method in Critical Media Literacy," *Postdigital Science and Education* (2020): 1–21.

[33] Some pictures can even interfere with effective information processing of associated information; for an example, consult Pascal Klein, Stefan Küchemann, Paul van Kampen, Leanne Doughty, and Jochen Kuhn, "Picture Bias in Upper-Division Physics Education," in *Frontiers and Advances in Positive Learning in the Age of InformaTiOn (PLATO)*, ed. O. Zlatkin-Troitschanskaia (Cham, Switzerland: Springer, 2019), 135–142.

own visual language to communicate and how the design choices employed in a work can influence that communication. Comparing an image to a text it purportedly illustrates can be incredibly effective way to show that even images that were designed to serve as illustrations still need close visual analysis. In my general education course on World Mythology in Art, I ask students to compare an image of Noah's ark, which served as an illustration in a manuscript of the bible,[34] to the text in Genesis. This comparison shows how textual ekphrasis and narrative must be translated into the visual format, as it simply is not possible for artists to depict everything described in the text—such as, for example, two of every animal—nor can artists show every moment from the building to the landing of the ark. It also shows how unremarked upon details in the text are translated by artists for their audience. This explains why these biblical figures are depicted ahistorically, often wearing ancient Roman clothes, as this was visual convention for indicating the remote past. One can also observe how the artist makes specific visual choices in the representation to convey information to the viewer. For example, in order to help viewers distinguish the figure of Noah from that of his sons, Noah is sometimes depicted as larger to show his importance, or with a longer beard to show his advanced age, or performing a well-known action, such as looking for the returning bird. This is why another effective assignment to focus on the impact of visual choices is to have students compare two images of the same subject. After these types of activities, it is not uncommon for students to tell me how much they learned about an image they originally thought was so simple and straightforward; in the words of one student, "I really thought I knew that image until I looked at it."

Here is a simple, general checklist that can be provided to students to help them look closely at images, although I often like to tailor the list to focus the questions more specifically to the image being examined:

- What information does the image provide about the setting of the image? What gives the viewer clues about the time and location where the image is set?
- Are there any recognizable figures or features within the image?
- Do there appear to be any recognizable signs or symbols employed in the work?
- How is the image arranged? What figures or features draw your eye due to visual elements such as scale (size in relation to other depicted figures and/or features), color, figures' gazes within the work, and pose? If you can pay attention to where your own eye is drawn in the work, you can spot directional forces being employed in the work (e.g., having a figure in the work point at another figure creates a line for the eye to follow)!

[34]There are many examples one can chose from online; the one I use comes from the 1495 illustration from the Nuremberg Bible.

- Does there appear to be some sort of narrative? Do you recognize the narrative? If so, how?
- What emotional impact do you think the work has on the viewer and why?
- Are there some unusual or distinctive elements in the work that you suspect may be related to a particular time and place of the work—understanding that the setting may be different from the origins of the work—or the artist who made the work? For the latter, consider use of color, surface treatment, and degree of visual clarity.

So, while it may be true that images speak for themselves to some degree, it is critically important to understand that hearing images effectively requires learning as much of their language as possible and listening intently! While I require very little use of specialized vocabulary in most of my art history courses, I often include terms in part of the discussion to show students how valuable some terms can be. For example, when discussing Greek temples, I talk about how they have columns all around the outside of the building, which can be abbreviated with the use of the term peripteral. I often refer to these specialized terms as "shortcuts" and note how they are also included and defined in the textbook in case students might want to use any of them to save time on our written slide exam. This more passive approach to vocabulary building does appear to have some effect, as some terms do appear in assessments—even if often misspelled—as well as other activities. At times, though, I will employ an activity that is designed to make students focus on some core art terms associated with the basic elements of visual description. For example, after taking about some essential elements and principles of deign in association with the visual analysis of a work, I sometimes ask students to take a picture of real-life objects that show the same application of some of those art term; I now call this activity "Art and Design All Around," after a student commented in the conclusion of her activity that she had never really noticed how there was art and design all around us all the time before this activity. It can also be useful to post some images on an online discussion board and ask students to make posts that identify and describe how an individual element and principle of design is being employed in the work; to motivate students to really push themselves to find less obvious terms used in the work, I prohibit the repetition of terms within a thread and assign ascending value to posts.

One of the aspects of visual analysis that will require the most repetition is that the practice of visual analysis is not grounded on what the viewer thinks or feels about the image. With Facebook and other social media platforms, student have been reinforced in the habit of "liking" images, which only serves to reinforce the idea that image evaluation is grounded in personal opinion;[35]

---

[35] Social opinion of images, products, and content unquestionably has an impact on users' behaviors, even if that impact is not always simplistic and straightforward; for example, see Shira Dvir-Gvirsman, "I Like What I See: Studying the Influence of Popularity Cues on Attention Allocation and News Selection," *Information, Communication & Society* 22, no. 2 (2019): 286–305.

also, since negative feedback on something presented by a peer can be socially problematic, students often tend to be particularly hesitant about statements that might be perceived as negative.[36] Therefore, it is particularly important to model effective critique practices for students and always support statements about the work by citing specific visual evidence from the work, as seen in the earlier characterization of the clocks in *The Persistence of Memory*. This is particularly important when making interpretations about a work, which is why I often like to remind students about the non-universality of perceptions. For example, to undermine the idea that black is always symbol for death, I will mention that while the Romans did establish a tradition that associates black clothes with mourning in many Western cultures, there are many other perspectives to consider; for example, Africans traditionally wear white to funerals, but wearing black outside of a funereal context can represent elegance and style in many cultures. Keep reminding students that they are welcome to personally like or enjoy any work they wish in their personal time, but that academic research can only be meaningful if the information and assumptions made are clearly stated and supported, which is also why source citation is so important to scholarly work.

Therefore, whenever students present opinions about a work in class, I will ask them to support it or, if the comment is not supportable, I will work to redirect it; in that latter case, I start by expressing how I can understand how the student came to that characterization, but then I will suggest some alternative interpretation, overlooked visual element, or contextual fact that would make their characterization less likely to be the one that was originally intended. This not only reinforces how statements drawn from visual evidence are different from opinion, but also provides a model for students who might want to suggest their own interpretation. Indeed, I will often display an image early in the semester knowing that it will trigger this type of discussion, such as an ancient Greek vase containing swastikas. I don't bother to point out this symbol myself, as someone in the class always does and, even better, another student in the class will note that the Nazis appropriated this ancient sun symbol. Still, these discussion strategies are only useful for relevant student remarks. When students make really off-topic comments—and I have found that images from other times and places generate a surprising amount of these—I will simply remark how while that brings up an interesting issue, we don't have time to address it properly in this class, but I would happily discuss the topic office hours or in an online discussion board. I always make sure to have a non-graded discussion board on our learning management system that can fit this purpose and I invite also students to make a reply to this board if they can answer another student's question. While I will admit this question and answer

---

[36] Students express great concern regarding the attitude and respectfulness of a peer critique, as evidenced in the study by Jiming Zhou, Yongyan Zheng, and Joanna Hong-Meng Tai, "Grudges and Gratitude: The Social-Affective Impacts of Peer Assessment," *Assessment & Evaluation in Higher Education* 45, no. 3 (2020): 345–358.

discussion board is more often filled with questions about course procedures, content, and activities—most of which I usually answer myself—some unexplored topics from class do appear periodically; one semester, after I showed the Greek vase with the swastika in class, there was a funny tongue-and-cheek discussion about time-traveling Nazis that eventually led to a much more serious discussion debunking other unfounded claims still circulating in popular media, such as aliens building the ancient Egyptian pyramids. Ultimately, though, I strongly encourage instructors to remain open to those questions that might provide them with a worthy opportunity to display to students how they themselves are lifelong learners; not a semester has gone by in my own career that I haven't had a student ask a question to which I've responded, "That's an excellent question to which I don't have a properly informed answer, so let me investigate it and I'll share my findings with you all at the start of our next class meeting."

Once students have built up some of their visual analysis skills, it can be very useful to provide students with some unillustrated information and ask them to find or create an image to accompany it. Having students present their choice—either in class or on a discussion board—is particularly useful for helping students see different solutions, as well as assessing each examples advantages and disadvantages. This type of activity is also a natural accompaniment to a traditional research paper, but it is critical that students are required to employ images as evidence within the paper and not simply as an illustration, so be sure to make the appropriateness of the selected images along with their effective use within the paper part of the criteria for evaluation. As I will discuss in a later chapter, it can be very useful to ask students to compare the images of the past to that of the present. Or, in place of a research paper, consider requiring a research poster. This option will probably be well-received by students even though it is much more challenging in practice, as it asks students to use text and image strategically and economically to explain and support their thesis. While this type of communication is common in digital environments, these skills are not a frequent focus within an academic environment.[37] Future chapters will provide even more examples of how students can interact actively and effectively with material culture that is outside of their own experience to support their own learning as well as that of their peers.

In summary, this chapter discussed the following approaches for making images an integral component of course content:

- Select images appropriate to the topic (see summary bullet points within chapter).
- Use an image to engage students during class (see summary bullet points within chapter)

---

[37] Tracey S. Hodges and Sharon D. Matthews, "Digital Literacies and Text Structure Instruction: Benefits, New Language Demands, and Changes to Pedagogy," in *Handbook of Research on Integrating Digital Technology with Literacy Pedagogies*, eds. Pamela M. Sullivan, Jessica L. Lantz, and Brian A. Sullivan (Hershey, Pennsylvania: IGI Global, 2020), 52–71.

- Post supporting content about images used during class on a learning management system; this posting can come from the instructor, or it can be something that involves students.
- Design an activity outside of class that asks students to closely analyze a single image or to contrast it to a textual account of the depicted event.
- Have students employ images within their written analysis of course content.
- Assess students' use of images in image-related activities, making sure to evaluate the degree to which specific elements within cited images were effectively employed to support points within the larger argument.

References

Archino, Sarah. "Addressing Visual Literacy in the Survey: Balancing Transdisciplinary Competencies and Course Content." *Art History Pedagogy & Practice* 5, no. 1 (2020): 1–14.

Bai, Qiyu, Qi Dan, Zhe Mu, and Maokun Yang. "A Systematic Review of Emoji: Current Research and Future Perspectives." *Frontiers in Psychology* 10 (2019): 1–16. https://www.frontiersin.org/articles/10.3389/fpsyg.2019.02221/full.

Bogre Michelle. *Documentary Photography Reconsidered: History, Theory and Practice* (New York: Routledge, 2020).

Büchele, Stefan. "Evaluating the Link Between Attendance and Performance in Higher Education: The Role of Classroom Engagement Dimensions." *Assessment & Evaluation in Higher Education* 46, no. 1 (2021): 132–150.

Carter, Christopher. *Rhetorical Exposures: Confrontation and Contradiction in US Social Documentary Photography* (Tuscaloosa: The University of Alabama Press, 2015).

Coffelt, Tina A, Dale Grauman, and Frances L. M. Smith. "Employers' Perspectives on Workplace Communication Skills: The Meaning of Communication Skills." *Business and Professional Communication Quarterly* 82, no. 4 (2019): 418–439.

Droney, Damien. "The Business of "Getting Up": Street Art and Marketing in Los Angeles." *Visual Anthropology* 23, no. 2 (2010): 98–114.

Dvir-Gvirsman, Shira. "I Like What I See: Studying the Influence of Popularity Cues on Attention Allocation and News Selection." *Information, Communication & Society* 22, no. 2 (2019): 286–305.

Evans, Chris and Wenqian Robertson. "The Four Phases of the Digital Natives Debate." *Human Behavior and Emerging Technologies* 2, no. 3 (2020): 269–277.

Fairey, Shepard. 1990. Manifesto. https://obeygiant.com/.

Fairey, Shepard. 2023. Obey Clothing. https://obeyclothing.com/.

Grant, Naomi K. and April L. McGrath. "Effects of PowerPoint Slides on Attendance and Learning: If You Share it, They Will (Still) Come." *Scholarship of Teaching and Learning in Psychology* (2021): 1–7. https://doi.org/10.1037/stl0000241.

Gwaltney, Kevin D. "General Education Requirements: A Look at the Structure of Higher Education." Missouri General Assembly Joint Committee on Education (August 19, 2020). http://www.senate.mo.gov/jced/GeneralEducationRequirementsRethinking theStructureofHigherEducation.pdf.

Hallewell, Madeline J. and Natasa Lackovic. "Do Pictures 'Tell' a Thousand Words in Lectures? How Lecturers Vocalise Photographs in Their Presentations." *Higher Education Research & Development* 36, no. 6 (2017): 1166–1180.

Herting, David Chávez, Ramón Cladellas Pros, and Antoni Castelló Tarrida. "Patterns of PowerPoint Use in Higher Education: A Comparison Between the Natural, Medical, and Social Sciences." *Innovative Higher Education* 45, no. 1 (2020): 65–80.

Hobbs, Victoria. "The Function of a 'Fetish' Figure." *V&A Conservation Journal 31* (1999). http://www.vam.ac.uk/content/journals/conservation-journal/issue-31/the-function-of-a-fetish-figure/.

Hodges, Tracey S. and Sharon D. Matthews. "Digital Literacies and Text Structure Instruction: Benefits, New Language Demands, and Changes to Pedagogy." In *Handbook of Research on Integrating Digital Technology with Literacy Pedagogies*, edited by Pamela M. Sullivan, Jessica L. Lantz, and Brian A. Sullivan, 52–71 (Hershey, PA: IGI Global, 2020).

Kidd, Jenny, Sam Cairns, Alex Drago, and Amy Ryall, eds. *Challenging History in the Museum: International Perspectives* (London: Routledge, 2016).

Klein, Pascal, Stefan Küchemann, Paul van Kampen, Leanne Doughty, and Jochen Kuhn. "Picture Bias in Upper-division Physics Education." *In Frontiers and Advances in Positive Learning in the Age of InformaTiOn (PLATO)*, edited by O. Zlatkin-Troitschanskaia, 135–142 (Cham, Switzerland: Springer, 2019).

Lackovic, Natasa. "Thinking with Digital Images in the Post-Truth Era: A Method in Critical Media Literacy." *Postdigital Science and Education* (2020): 1–21.

Lazard, Allison J., Mary A. Bock, and Michael S. Mackert. "Impact of Photo Manipulation and Visual Literacy on Consumers' Responses to Persuasive Communication." *Journal of Visual Literacy* 39, no. 2 (2020): 90–110.

Martzoukou, Konstantina, Crystal Fulton, Petros Kostagiolas, and Charilaos Lavranos. "A Study of Higher Education Students' Self-Perceived Digital Competences for Learning and Everyday Life Online Participation." *Journal of Documentation* 76, no. 6 (2020): 1413–1458.

Miller, Amy Chasteen and Brooklyn Mills. "'If They Don't Care, I Don't Care': Millennial and Generation Z Students and the Impact of Faculty Caring." *Journal of the Scholarship of Teaching and Learning* 19, no. 4 (2019): 78–89.

MoMA Highlights: 375 Works from The Museum of Modern Art. New York: The Museum of Modern Art, 2019. https://www.moma.org/collection/works/79018.

Muenks, Katherine, Elizabeth A. Canning, Jennifer LaCosse, Dorainne J. Green, Sabrina Zirkel, Julie A. Garcia, and Mary C. Murphy. "Does my Professor Think my Ability Can Change? Students' Perceptions of Their STEM Professors' Mindset Beliefs Predict Their Psychological Vulnerability, Engagement, and Performance in Class." *Journal of Experimental Psychology: General* 149, no. 11 (2020): 2119–2144.

Roberts, David. "The Engagement Agenda, Multimedia Learning and the Use of Images in Higher Education Lecturing: or, How to End Death by PowerPoint." *Journal of Further and Higher Education* 42, no. 7 (2018): 969–985.

Rose, Gillian. *Visual Methodologies: An Introduction to Researching with Visual Materials*. 4th ed. (London: Sage, 2016).

Szafir, Danielle Albers. "The Good, the Bad, and the Biased: Five Ways Visualizations Can Mislead (and How to Fix Them)." *Interactions* 25, no. 4 (2018): 26–33.

Swan, Glenda. "Building a Foundation for Survey: Employing a Focused Introduction." *Art History Pedagogy & Practice* (2016): 1–18. https://academicworks.cuny.edu/cgi/viewcontent.cgi?article=1001&context=ahpp.

Tavin, Kevin. "Heidi Cody: Letters to the world and the ABCs of visual culture." In *Culture as Commons: Art and Social Justice Education*, edited by Therese M. Quinn, John Ploof and Lisa J. Hochtritt, 9–10 (New York: Routledge, 2012).

Thompson, Dana Statton. "Recommended Reads for Visual Literacy: An Online Bibliography of Articles, Books, and Archival Materials." *Art Documentation: Journal of the Art Libraries Society of North America* 39, no. 2 (2020): 239–246.

Winterhalter, Teresa. "Desire Under the Lens: Critical Perspective in a Duane Michals Photograph." *Literature and Theology* 11, no. 3 (1997): 229–38.

Yarosh, Jerrod H. "The Syllabus Reconstructed: An Analysis of Traditional and Visual Syllabi for Information Retention and Inclusiveness." *Teaching Sociology* 49, no. 2 (2021): 173–183.

Zhou, Jiming, Yongyan Zheng, and Joanna Hong-Meng Tai. "Grudges and Gratitude: The Social-Affective Impacts of Peer Assessment." *Assessment & Evaluation in Higher Education* 45, no. 3 (2020): 345–358.

CHAPTER 3

The Past Is the New Present

Like Janus, the Roman god of doorways, I am very comfortable having one face that looks behind while the other that looks forward. The past provides all of us with some larger perspectives that help us to understand the time and place in which we live as well as the perspectives of other people within that shared culture. My training as an archeologist has taught me that time changes not only what we see, but also how we interpret what we find.[1] Indeed, understanding how to approach the past has led me to reflect more on the present, as I have to recognize my own assumptions and biases to make sure I am viewing the evidence of the material past with more clear eyes.[2] As you might imagine, this involves the type of reflection that is too often missing from the personally directed content that is immediately available at any time and in any place.[3] However, after establishing the value and usefulness of this type of simultaneous contemplation of past and present in my courses, I have discovered that many students have found that past can be a useful doorway to the future for themselves as well.

This connection between past and present is critically important to my teaching, as I do not teach students who are focused on the study of the material culture of the past, despite the fact that it is my academic specialty; there is no Classical Studies program or major in art history at my institution, and I teach general education students or majors in contemporary studio art, art

---

[1] There are many texts on the changes in archeological practices and methodologies over time, but to reflect even more deeply on this topic, see Rachel J. Crellin, *Change and Archaeology* (New York: Routledge, 2020).

[2] For evidence of how this approach is transferable and effective to other fields, consult Amy Zeidan et al., "Targeting implicit bias in medicine: lessons from art and archaeology," *Western Journal of Emergency Medicine* 21, no. 1 (2020): 1–3.

[3] The amount of immediate information modern technology provides can interfere with sustained focused thinking, as discussed by Pablo J. Boczkowski, *Abundance: On the Experience of Living in a World of Information Plenty* (New York: Oxford University Press, 2021).

© The Author(s), under exclusive license to Springer Nature Switzerland AG 2023

G. Swan, *ReEnvisioning the Material Past,*
https://doi.org/10.1007/978-3-031-24027-0_3

education, or interior design. Because I am always teaching to non-specialists—even if that teaching occurs in different contexts and at different levels—I understand that my core pedagogical goals in every course are to explain how the material I teach is relevant to the students taking it as well as to make them feel confident that they will be able to master that material.[4] Achieving these goals certainly involves active learning practices that will be addressed in future chapters, but much of it also involves a foundational perspective about how course information is presented and discussed with students.[5] I treat them as partners in the process of their own learning and share much of the same information about the proven importance of visual analysis that was the subject of the second chapter of this book. I make it clear that I do not assume that they are specialists in this area or, for some courses, to have had any previous exposure to the subject, but that I do require them to engage with activities and resources that have been specifically designed and organized to help them achieve course success and learn valuable transferable skills, such as visual analysis. While they can expect that I will regularly share useful approaches and strategies with them, I expect them to share what is helping and what is interfering with their learning with me in return—possibly during the course, but certainly in the student evaluations at the end of the semester. For while I have worked hard to design a clear, effective, and well-organized course,[6] my ultimate role can only be as a facilitator of student learning.[7] This reorientation of perspective on traditional classroom roles is one of the first ways that I try to start teaching students to think about the world around them from a new perspective.

Looking at the multitude of contexts that are associated with images is beneficial not simply to visual analysis, but also in getting students to think very about things from the perspective of others, which is itself important to have a meaningful understanding of diversity. Personally, I like to address diversity as a positive aspect of our classroom from the first day of class.[8] I note how

[4] Both of these aspects are important to student achievement of learning outcomes, as demonstrated in the student by Chris S. Hulleman et al, "Making connections: Replicating and extending the utility value intervention in the classroom," *Journal of Educational Psychology* 109, no. 3 (2017): 387–404.

[5] My own teaching philosophy is strongly aligned with the goals of "Transparency in Learning and Teaching (TILT)" and information and resources about it can be found online at https://tilthighered.com/.

[6] Because I employ a variety of pedagogical approaches in any course, it is critical that I establish and maintain a clear and solid foundation for my courses. For a useful recent reflection regarding such "basics" of course design, see Charles Blaich, "Clear and Organized Teaching: Simple in Concept, but Hard in Practice," *New Directions for Teaching and Learning* 164 (2020): 9–17.

[7] Of course, being a facilitator involves many different roles that vary in response to student needs, which is why I have found Student-Centered Learning and Teaching (SCLT) to be a useful characterization of much of my own teaching; for more about this pedagogical approach, see Sabine Hoidn and Manja Klemenčič, eds., *The Routledge International Handbook of Student-Centered Learning and Teaching in Higher Education* (New York: Routledge, 2020).

[8] Inclusive teaching is a core principle of my pedagogy, as I detail in the two chapters contributed to Lavonna L. Lovern, *Fostering a Climate of Inclusion in the College Classroom: The Missing Voice of the Humanities* (Cham, Switzerland: Springer, 2018).

everyone has a variety of different identities and associations: diversity of backgrounds, knowledge, perspectives, interests, and so on. I then explain how our primary role in this classroom requires that all of us—including me—must first be good learners and not be afraid to ask questions so we can gain more appreciation not only of other perspectives into course content, but also of the diversity within the course content itself. Then, I show a well-known work, such as an Egyptian pyramid, and ask student to think about the view of the leader who paid to have the work made, the people who designed and built the work, the audience that would have seen the work at the time it was made, as well as all the people who have continued to view it long after the work was made. This, I argue, is part of what makes the study of art interesting: a work that may have been looked at many times can still be seen in a new way. I then like to show a later image that referenced the image in some way, such as the glass pyramids at the entrance to the Louvre, and ask students to consider the impact of that visual reference on modern viewers. How were architect I. M. Pei's structures designed to inspire viewers look at the past in a new way while still keeping the idea of the museum as a place for preserving the relics of the past? Why do you think that they are an oft-cited feature of Paris today, but were very unpopular when the design was first made public in 1985?[9]

It is useful to explain to students how many of the artworks and monuments that are valued today were not always seen as being particularly special. I like to tell my students that most ancient works were valued in a very practical way: the cost of materials and the amount of labor time that was put into the piece. Since pigments were made from ground minerals, some colors were valued more simply because they cost more. The impact of the amount of time spent on making a work had as much impact then as it has today; for example, in addition to seeing the clear difference in time that was spent on the same scenes and motifs painted walls of different houses at Pompeii, one can also visit modern websites that discuss the value the artist's labor in association with the price a painted portrait. Of course, while some works will become famous long after they were made, other works that were once lauded as masterworks will end up falling out of favor. A great example is the Apollo Belvedere, which was not a famous work when it was made, but it was celebrated as one of the greatest sculptures of antiquity during the revival of classicism in the late eighteenth and early nineteenth centuries, and then became an object of disdain in the twentieth century.[10] Works like this are useful for discussing the various ways in which people can relate to images. For example, because the classical style was gaining popularity in the mid-eighteenth century, it is not surprising that an ancient

---

[9] To learn more about this work, a useful online article is Elizabeth Evitts Dickinson, "Louvre Pyramid. The Folly that Became a Triumph," *Architect* (April 19, 2017), https://www.architect-magazine.com/awards/aia-honor-awards/louvre-pyramid-the-folly-that-became-a-triumph_o.

[10] For information about the reception of the Apollo Belvedere as well as other famous works, consult John Nici, *Famous Works of Art – And How They Got That Way* (Lanham, Maryland: Rowman & Littlefield, 2015).

work was viewed so positivity by leading critics of that time, as people react more positively images to which they feel they can relate. This is why avant-garde works are often not widely appreciated at the time they are made, as it can take time for most viewers to understand how they can relate to something that is truly new and different. I find that students are often very reflective and perceptive in these types of discussion about reception, context, and changing notions of value, as it often relates to many of their own experiences with trends within social media.

Such multiplicities of perspectives are not only vital in promoting a respectful classroom environment, but also an essential element to promoting critical thinking skills in students who have been trained to provide a single, correct answer to a question that often comes from memorization rather than analysis. Indeed, at the beginning of the course, it is not uncommon after a lively class discussion for a student to ask me, "So who had the right answer?" This question always provides a great opportunity to engage in a dialog about how knowledge is constructed within the classroom setting, reinforcing both our roles and responsibilities as co-learners to support interpretations with reasonable associations specific to the work. Of course, within a specific historical framework, some answers are unquestionably more correct than others, but students frequently lack specific knowledge of the political, social, historical, or artistic knowledge of a work's original context. Therefore, I will always make sure to kindly point out when a student has unintentionally interpreted an image from the past using the eyes of the present. I like to remind students frequently that they have been well-trained in how to memorize, but now they need to work on how to gather and evaluate data in an area which they probably had little or no training: images. I tell them that this skill takes time and effort to develop, so mistakes are not only to be expected, but often prove to be the most impactful and educational.

It is both useful and entertaining to have students talk about how naturally biased everyone is when viewing their own culture, as well as how cultures practices outside of one's normal experience are viewed as strange. I will often start by contributing something from my own personal history, including the fact that I never traveled outside of the region of my birth until after I started attending college. By sharing how my own early travel experience was similar to most of my students, this lessens their embarrassment for not being well-traveled and, I hope, will also fuel their own desire to travel. I certainly have many examples from which to draw, but I often like to discuss the notion of the *riposo*, or midday Italian break, as something that I hated as a tourist but came to really love once I spent some time living there. Students will often start with some examples from southern culture that do not translate outside the region, such as ordering tea and then getting hot rather than iced tea. A few students will even have some examples from their experiences traveling outside of America, although it is always the contributions by our international students that typically make the most impact, as it reminds students of the diversity that exists within our own classroom.

Disjunctions between past and present are also similarly fruitful sources for class discussion. For example, body image is an issue that students are intimately familiar, but they are rarely appreciative of how much the notion of that idea has varied in different places at different times. Personally, I like to compare an Egyptian pharaoh and an Archaic Greek kouros; while the Greek work was directly modeled from the Egyptian, it still makes critical cultural changes, which makes it a particularly ideal comparison. While students will often start by mentioning the difference in color, this presents me with an ideal opportunity to discuss the non-universality of color perceptions; for Egyptians, black would have been associated with the blossoming of agricultural life from the dark silt of the Nile and symbolized rebirth after death, while the Greek work would have been painted to make it more lifelike and memorable, either as a marker for a grave or as a temple dedication. This discussion also provides an opportunity to touch on the racist afterlife of some these notions of color usage, such as the love for the "pure white" statues of Greece, despite the fact that they were originally painted. The nakedness of the Greek figure is also useful for discussing the role of heroic nudity in ancient art, which I like to relate to students experience by referencing the armored chest-piece of comic-book heroes such as Batman, as well as issues of gender that come from the modern discomfort with male nudity in comparison to that of women in art.

Even just the straightforward presentation of the social, economic, or political contexts of older images is sometimes enough to shock students into reflecting on things from a different perspective. Pre-modern art is rife with examples that demonstrate how the individual artist or worker is unimportant; these works are made exclusively to meet the needs and goals of the person who has power and money to commission the work. How works expressing the power of the ruling class—as well as, at times, divine sanctioning of this unequal status quo—form the primary focus of many ancient works. This de-emphasis on traits that today's students hold so dear, such as individuality and personal expression, tends to leave a strong impression on students. The adoption of the masculine form by the female pharaoh Hatshepsut—as the power to rule in Egypt was communicated, in part, by an idealized make body because that was the traditional gender of the pharaoh—is a particularly potent example.[11] The study of these issues exerts a clear impact on students' abilities in the analysis of images as, over the course of the semester, students become more effective at identifying underlying power structures behind works as well as making increasing subtle analogies to continuing modern practices. For example, by the time of the midterm, it was not uncommon for students to make a comparison to how modern American leaders presented themselves in media. However, by grounding this practice so effectively in regard to past image-making, such connections with similar modern materials seemed natural rather than partisan

---

[11] Issues of gender, of course, impact not simply the art of Hatshepsut, but how her materials have been studied by scholars, as discussed in Kelly-Anne Diamond, "Hatshepsut: Transcending Gender in Ancient Egypt," *Gender & History* 32, no. 1 (2020): 168–188.

or politically motivated. While I know that many of my students had strong feelings about the 2016 election, personal positions were not expressed during our class discussion, although some interesting points were made about how the role of the president was gendered male in a number of ways; one student even compared Hillary Clinton's ubiquitous pantsuits to Hatshepsut's adoption of the male form.

Sometimes it is also useful to discuss how ancient cultures have misunderstood each other so that students can begin to examine how they see the world without confronting that worldview directly. For example, Roman views of early Christianity are always quite revelatory to students, who typically imagine the Christians as completely hidden out of fear of immediate persecution.[12] Recasting Romans as reluctant bureaucrats who were mainly interested in preserving law and order when faced with obvious—and sometimes irrational—opposition is useful for having students look more objectively at belief system with which they are very familiar without feeling challenged or attacked. Also, by putting the focus on how and why Christ was being represented by worshippers at that time requires that students focus on the visual manifestation of the religious belief system of that time rather than their own.[13] Indeed, by the time I pose the question, "Why did Christians become such an effective and, eventually, dominate belief structure in the Roman Empire," I have never had students attribute it to the power of Christ, even though many of my students might have previously been inclined to view the material from that type of personal perspective. I always make sure to discuss all religions in my class in the same manner, explaining how those belief and practices were understood and integrated into the culture of which they were a part without any type of value judgment. This approach not only allows me to de-sensationalize and contextualize practices such as human sacrifice in Aztec culture, but also makes it clear that the beliefs of any particular culture are discussed and analyzed from the same perspective as all other cultures and not from one's own perspective.

While I have found it very helpful for students to experience the discomfort that often comes with seeing things from a new perspective,[14] I do not want them feeling judged or belittled. This is not a simple task—particularly because it requires constant vigilance—but there are some approaches that can help create the right environment. Allot some time at the start of the course to discussions and activities that establish the tone of the classroom and promote

---

[12] The art of the Roman Catacombs is often said to be where Christians hid themselves and/or their religious worship, but an analysis of the larger context of these spaces reveals the shared social geography of these spaces by Christians, pagans, and Jews; more detailed discussion on this topic can be found in Laurie Brink and Deborah Green, eds., *Commemorating the Dead: Texts and Artifacts in Context. Studies of Roman, Jewish and Christian Burials* (Berlin: De Gruyter, 2008).

[13] For a discussion of the early images of Jesus and their relationship to art, religion, and culture, see Robin Margaret Jensen, *Understanding Early Christian Art* (London: Routledge, 2013).

[14] For more about this idea, see Iza Kavedzija, "Learning Discomfort," *Teaching Anthropology* 8, no. 1 (2019): 57–63.

productive peer conversations;[15] this is especially critical before engaging in projects that rely on effective student collaboration. Reflect on how course activities might be designed or evaluated in a manner that might mitigate social anxiety.[16] To the degree you feel is appropriate, consider involving students directly in helping to create that model; for example, in an upper-division art history course about gender, I used a recent online article called "How Calling on Random Students Could Hurt Women" to start a dialog about how we show hold discussions in our own course.[17] Monitor not simply the tone and phrasing of your corrective responses, but also your larger mindset.[18] Be aware of implicit biases—your own, your students', and the institution's.[19] People who become professionals in their field are usually extremely good students, so one's own past academic experience is usually not a reasonable expectation. Also, always remember how course performance can be impacted significantly by issues outside of the classroom. Of course, that doesn't mean it isn't useful to plan ahead to try and counteract common classroom issues. For example, I have found that putting up a slide with reminders about upcoming readings, activities, and/or events in the five minutes before as well as at the end of every class has eliminated the request for this information during actual class time.

I sometimes also find it useful to prepare in advance for a discussion of what I know to be potentially controversial content. For example, I always pre-plan my approach for the discussion of the building of the pyramids because it the first time that ancient slavery will be addressed in the class, and I want to pre-clude students from volunteering historically inaccurate connections with the Old Testament. Also, as someone who has regularly taught in Southern universities, I know that the word slavery immediately conjures a specific and highly charged image in the minds of students. So, I start by addressing some of the mistaken assumptions about the building of the pyramids, beginning in a light-hearted way with their connections to aliens before transitioning into images that show how new archeological investigations have clearly revealed that

[15] One can even talk about talking very directly; see Ruth M. C. Newman, "Engaging talk: one teacher's scaffolding of collaborative talk," *Language and Education* 31, no. 2 (2017): 130–151.

[16] See Matthew Cohen et al., "Think, pair, freeze: The association between social anxiety and student discomfort in the active learning environment," *Scholarship of Teaching and Learning in Psychology* 5, no. 4 (2019): 265–277.

[17] Beckie Supiano, "How Calling on Random Students Could Hurt Women," *The Chronicle of Higher Education*, August 15, 2019, https://www.chronicle.com/newsletter/teaching/2019-08-15.

[18] There is a lot of scholarship about how instructors' beliefs about teaching, learning, and the abilities of students can impact students' learning, but an article on this topic that also discusses the potential usefulness of errors is Steven C. Pan et al., "Learning from errors: students' and instructors' practices, attitudes, and beliefs," *Memory* 28, no. 9 (2020): 1105–1122.

[19] While much of the literature on this subject focuses on race and gender, there are many aspects of identity that can trigger bias, but all the literature agrees that the first step in working to correct biases is to become aware of them.

well-compensated, off-season labor of free men built the pyramids.[20] I explain that while Egypt—like most ancient cultures—practiced slavery, it was not the same as the race-based slavery found in antebellum America. I work to direct class discussion toward the larger idea that our role in this course is to neither idealize nor condemn past cultures, but to try and understand their worldview in order to make meaningful insights into their art and architecture. I have found that this managed discussion serves as a model that helps to sets the tone for how sensitive topics will be approached in the course and accustom students to setting aside their personal assumptions about course material.

At times, though, I will sometimes share my own personal experiences with the class; today's students respond particularly well to personal stories, although it is very important to make sure that any presented story is both relevant and appropriate.[21] For example, rather than tell the students in abstract about how they should avoid romanticizing the past, I have a personal story that I find helpful for contrasting an idealized view of the past with actual social practices that also carries a message about diversity. I was a volunteer cataloging pottery at an archeological dig in Southern Italy as an undergraduate when someone brought in fragment of pottery that appeared as though it may have been imported from Athens. Another student volunteer began rhapsodizing about how wonderful it would have been to live in the golden age of Greece and share in the conversations that formed the foundations of democracy. When he then asked me if I would like to travel back there as well, I said that while I love the art of Classical Athens, I would not want to go back to that time, as not only my gender would have prevented my participation in political affairs, but I probably would have had to spend most of my time in the women's quarters of the house. The other student paused, smiled, and replied that it was indeed important to not to forget all the advantages of the present, such indoor plumbing, to which I smiled and agreed in return. This story is meaningful to me not only because my peer acknowledged my feelings of difference in a kind and generous way, but also because this story reflects the type of atmosphere I work to foster in my classroom.

At times it can also be useful to make a reference directly to the present in order that students can relate more effectively to the past topic being discussed. For example, I have tried to convey the emotional impact of Persian destruction of the Acropolis in Athens by referencing the feeling invoked by the destruction brought by foreign terrorists to American soil on September 11, 2001; in both instances there also appeared to be some debate about that loss should be properly memorialized. I have also characterized the cathedrals that spring up all over in Europe during the Romanesque as being due to "Y1K" to

---

[20] Eric Betz, "Who Built the Egyptian Pyramids? Not Slaves," *Discovery Magazine*, February 1, 2021, https://www.discovermagazine.com/planet-earth/who-built-the-egyptian-pyramids-not-slaves.

[21] The effectiveness of this technique along with some cautions is discussed in R. Eric Landrum, Karen Brakke, and Maureen A. McCarthy, "The pedagogical power of storytelling," *Scholarship of Teaching and Learning in Psychology* 5, no. 3 (2019): 247–253.

help students understand its relationship to millennialism. I have compared the copying of the hairstyles of Roman leaders by regular Roman citizens with similar modern practices involving figures such as First Lady Jacqueline Kennedy, Princess Diana of Wales, and actress Jennifer Aniston. The fact that I no longer use any of these examples is evidence of how important it is to seek well-known and recognizable examples, as references to "contemporary" events and people fall out of relevance much more quickly than you may suspect.

Yet even when my own discussion remains exclusively grounded and focused on the past, many connections between socio-political issues of the past and the present are so obvious that I do not bother to reference them directly; in these instances, it is not uncommon that a student will volunteer a comment that makes some connection to modern art or society. For example, in a discussion of the notion of ideal motherhood that was consciously constructed during the Enlightenment period, the ongoing impact of this idea in modern society clearly resonated with many of my Gender in Art students. In addition to a lively discussion during our class meeting, some students even circulated images from modern media with the other members of the class using a class email list. Inspired by student interest in the topic, I designed an assignment for an online discussion next time I offered the class; the assignment required students to compare an eighteenth-century work depicting an idealized mother from an assigned academic article to an image of contemporary motherhood and then discuss a significant point of similarity or difference between the two images. While I was expecting lots of similarities with advertisements of products associated with babies and/or Mother's Day gifts—and there were some of those—I was surprised at the number of students that explored a difference that was then linked with a more socio-political issue, such as public breastfeeding or the lack of support provided to American mothers in the labor force. Working at a southern regional university where feminist is considered an undesirable label among most of our students, I must admit that I was quite surprised by these posts. It was as if the controversial nature of these observations were somehow blunted because of the connection that was being made with the past. Moreover, student evaluations of instruction that semester did not seem negatively impacted when compared to earlier offerings of the course. I think that by leaving the question open and allowing the students to make the connections themselves, they did not feel as though I was pushing some sort of agenda.

One semester I even took a poll of my students in Art History I class, which involves a survey of world cultures that starts in the Paleolithic and ends right before the Renaissance, and asked, "Do you think the material in this course has caused you to reflect on any modern social and/or political issues?" In response, 76% of the students in the course responded that it did either "Frequently" or "Sometimes." Some of the comments included with those categorizations were as follows:

- This course makes you look back and reflect on past cultures, compare them to now, and see similarities between the cultures and your own worldview.
- The materials in this course have really highlighted the social/cultural/political connectedness we experience as humans. No culture or society isolated. As Americans especially we influence and are influenced by all other nations.
- There are times in this class that you can see how history has repeated itself and evolved into today's society.

This poll solidified my thinking about the relevance of the past to contemporary students and I more fully appreciated why student feedback on the end of semester opinions of student instruction often mentioned how they enjoyed the class even though they "had no interest in the topic." Today's students are not predisposed to think they will learn anything interesting from the study of the past, so when they do discover connections to their contemporary life and interests, it really surprises them.

In summary, this chapter focused on connecting older images with modern content and made the following recommendations:

- Make students active collaborators in their own learning and ask for their help in connecting objects from the past with contemporary life.
- Exploit the inherent variety and flexibility within visual communication to educate students in issues of diversity, equity, and inclusion.
- Share a variety of interpretations to show how there can be more than one path to understanding the complexities of material culture.
- Regularly reinforce the idea that visual analysis is not a traditional area of education outside of academia, so mistakes are to be expected—and so instructors should feel free to share some of their own—but it is a skill that can be learned.
- Find examples that will confound student expectations to make them appreciate how much images can hide in plain sight if they are not subjected to informed looking.
- Remind students that material culture was usually designed to speak to a specific audience, so miscommunication is to be expected from viewers not a part of that original audience, which led to some works having an "afterlife" that may be very different from their original one.
- The process of learning can be emotional, especially when it involves working with others. Work regularly on building a positive and supportive classroom environment and preplan for the delivery of emotionally challenging course content.
- Understand that study of the past is always undertaken in relation to the present. Share some of your own thoughts and experiences in relation to course content and invite students to do the same.

REFERENCES

Betz, Eric. "Who Built the Egyptian Pyramids? Not Slaves." *Discovery Magazine.* February 1, 2021. https://www.discovermagazine.com/planet-earth/who-built-the-egyptian-pyramids-not-slaves.

Blaich, Charles. "Clear and Organized Teaching: Simple in Concept, but Hard in Practice." *New Directions for Teaching and Learning* 164 (2020): 9–17.

Boczkowski, Pablo J. *Abundance: On the Experience of Living in a World of Information Plenty* (New York: Oxford University Press, 2021).

Brink, Laurie and Deborah Green, eds. *Commemorating the Dead: Texts and Artifacts in Context. Studies of Roman, Jewish and Christian Burials* (Berlin: De Gruyter, 2008).

Cohen, Matthew, Steven G. Buzinski, Emma Armstrong-Carter, Jenna Clark, Benjamin Buck, and Lillian Reuman. "Think, Pair, Freeze: The Association Between Social Anxiety and Student Discomfort in the Active Learning Environment." *Scholarship of Teaching and Learning in Psychology* 5, no. 4 (2019): 265–277.

Crellin, Rachel J. *Change and Archaeology* (New York: Routledge, 2020).

Diamond, Kelly-Anne. "Hatshepsut: Transcending Gender in Ancient Egypt." *Gender & History* 32, no. 1 (2020): 168–188.

Dickinson, Elizabeth Evitts. "Louvre Pyramid: The Folly That Became a Triumph." *Architect.* April 19, 2017. https://www.architectmagazine.com/awards/aia-honor-awards/louvre-pyramid-the-folly-that-became-a-triumph_o.

Hoidn, Sabine and Manja Klemenčič, eds. *The Routledge International Handbook of Student-Centered Learning and Teaching in Higher Education* (New York: Routledge, 2020).

Hulleman, Chris S., Jeff J. Kosovich, Kenneth E. Barron, and David B. Daniel. "Making Connections: Replicating and Extending the Utility Value Intervention in the Classroom." *Journal of Educational Psychology* 109, no. 3 (2017): 387–404.

Jensen, Robin Margaret. *Understanding Early Christian Art* (London: Routledge, 2013).

Kavedzija, Iza. "Learning Discomfort." *Teaching Anthropology* 8, no. 1 (2019): 57–63.

Landrum, R. Eric, Karen Brakke, and Maureen A. McCarthy. "The Pedagogical Power of Storytelling." *Scholarship of Teaching and Learning in Psychology* 5, no. 3 (2019): 247–253.

Lovern, Lavonna L. *Fostering a Climate of Inclusion in the College Classroom: The Missing Voice of the Humanities* (Cham, Switzerland: Springer, 2018).

Newman, Ruth M. C. "Engaging Talk: One Teacher's Scaffolding of Collaborative Talk." *Language and Education* 31, no. 2 (2017): 130–151.

Nici, John. *Famous Works of Art – And How They Got That Way* (Lanham, MD: Rowman & Littlefield, 2015).

Pan, Steven C. Faria Sana, Joshua Samani, James Cooke, and Joseph A. Kim. "Learning from Errors: Students' and Instructors' Practices, Attitudes, and Beliefs." *Memory* 28, no. 9 (2020): 1105–1122.

Supiano, Beckie. "How Calling on Random Students Could Hurt Women." *The Chronicle of Higher Education.* August 15, 2019. https://www.chronicle.com/newsletter/teaching/2019-08-15.

Zeidan, Amy, Anne Tiballi, Melanie Woodward, and Isha Marina Di Bartolo. "Targeting Implicit Bias in Medicine: Lessons from Art and Archaeology." *Western Journal of Emergency Medicine* 21, no. 1 (2020): 1–3.

CHAPTER 4

New Approaches for Old Material

There is an abundance of scholarship that stresses the effectiveness of both project-based learning and problem-based learning.[1] However, accessible undergraduate curricula using these approaches are limited, and there are even fewer that focus on the past and can be run by a single instructor as a unit within established courses.[2] For these reasons, I have found creating my own units—and even my own courses—most effectively allows students to engage actively with the material culture of the past, particularly that which forms the basis of my own specialized study as an academic. Fortunately, I have also learned that students do not need to be experts to engage with specialized material if the instructor has designed the course appropriately and effectively. This chapter will contain a number of specific examples from several different courses, but I wanted to discuss those examples within the context of each course so that readers might also gain insight into the larger development and design of these courses as well as the approaches and activities employed within them.

[1] While Project-Based Learning is not identical to Problem-Based Learning in its process or outcomes, the overall effectiveness of both in improving students' critical thinking has been summarized recently in a literature review by Muhammad Hafeez, "Systematic review on modern learning approaches, critical thinking skills and students learning outcomes," *Indonesian Journal of Educational Research and Review* 4, no. 1 (2021): 167–178.

[2] There are some very good game-based group projects, but they often require time, money, and other types of support to operate that many instructors do not have. However, instructors interested in the impact of incorporating "gamification" elements into existing course content should consult the recent literary survey by Rui Huang et al., "The impact of gamification in educational settings on student learning outcomes: a meta-analysis," *Educational Technology Research and Development* 68, no. 4 (2020): 1875–1901.

© The Author(s), under exclusive license to Springer Nature Switzerland AG 2023
G. Swan, *ReEnvisioning the Material Past,*
https://doi.org/10.1007/978-3-031-24027-0_4

Roman Life in Pompeii

The idea for my Roman Life at Pompeii course began as I spoke with my colleagues to see what upper-division topic course might serve our majors in interior design, art education, and studio art most effectively outside of contemporary art. The universal response I received was that the survey course I offered satisfied the specific level of content about ancient required by the overseeing accreditation programs for all those areas. The hard skills of research, critical thinking, and writing were all mentioned by my colleagues as ones that they knew would already be a focus of any advanced art history course, but they also cited their students' need for soft skills such as effective communication, teamwork, time management, and adaptability both before and after graduation. This focus on skills seemed particularly appropriate to the course since it would be populated by art majors with no previous content knowledge of Classical culture other than the survey course, which was the only prerequisite. Course content clearly needed to be presented with the goal of meeting larger learning goals.

With this in mind, I reflected upon what I could easily adapt from my own knowledge base that would allow students as much direct interaction with that material as possible. One of my personal academic specialties is in the study of Pompeii, which was extraordinarily well-preserved by the eruption of Mt. Vesuvius in 79 CE. The amount of preserved material would not only allow students to better envision the material culture of the ancient past, but also be useful in teaching them to understand how the interpretation of those remains is critical to understanding life in Pompeii before the eruption. I wanted to place the focus less on detailed content knowledge about Pompeii itself—as none of my students would ever need to employ such knowledge—and more on what Pompeii could teach students about how design could be employed to support the function of spaces as well as communicate on a social, political, and economic level to viewers.

The first step was determining what knowledge students would need to be able to recall without accessing any supporting materials or, in other words, what working foundation of facts would allow for more clear and meaningful discussion of context and interpretation. I realized that I was important for students to have a general sense of Pompeii's history as an Italic settlement, a Roman colony, and an Imperial town; for that reason, I decided that an assessment would employ a simple map of Pompeii as well as some questions about key structures, with the focus being on the reason for construction of those buildings along with how and why they changed during each of those major periods of Pompeii's history. I also needed students to understand the physical and culture role of the Roman house and the four styles of Roman wall-painting; so, again, I decided I would include a plan of the rooms of the Roman house and their idealized arrangement as well as some questions on selected well-known houses to promote more discussion of the structure and décor of actual Pompeian houses. The maps, plans, and specific structures were provided to students in a study guide along with examples of those assessments and suggestions for how to study for both. For the first assessment, I recommended that students make a notecard for each structure listed on the study guide that focused on each structure's location within the city as well as a summary of the status of the structure in its pre-Roman, Roman Republic and Imperial periods (as applicable). For the second assessment, I recommended that students make notecards that listed the rooms and their idealized arrangement within the house so they could label them, described the four styles of Roman painting so that they would be able to identify them, and summarized the décor and plan for each named house listed on the study guide.

The final planned assessment would need to cover some of the other many potential elements of life at Pompeii, such as roads, water, latrines, tombs, cult practices, shops, inns, brothels, wine, bread, textile industry, and so on. I decided that these subjects would be ideal topics for student research. In the selection of topics with useful bibliographic support, I was inspired by the table of contents in *The World of Pompeii*[3] and, since the book provides and overview along with specific bibliographic sources on those topics, I placed on library reserve and recommended it as a first source for all research. After the assignation of topics from ranked listing of student preferences, students would research their topic with the goal of selecting a physical object and/or space from Pompeii that effectively represents their specific investigation into their topic and would serve as a required slide for the final. At the end of the semester, students would need to teach the rest of the class about their topic, while a formal research paper would be submitted only to me, presentation and summary materials would be shared with fellow students through our online learning management system. All students would then be assessed on the material presented and shared by their peers on the final exam.

Of course, by integrating student research into course content, it was crucial to guide and support students throughout the entire process.[4] I made a variety of research and writing support materials available through the class learning management system. The required submission of certain in-process materials over the course of the semester would help keep students on track and allow me and/or peers to provide formative feedback. However, I also allotted class time to discuss research, writing, and presentation methods in class.[5] I even assigned myself a topic—the production of the fermented fish condiment,

---

[3] J. Dobbins and Pedar W. Foss, eds., *The World of Pompeii* (New York: Routledge, 2007).

[4] For a more detailed discussion about how to support and incorporate student research into a course, see Glenda Swan, "Integrating Student Research into Course Content," *Engaged Student Learning: Essays on Best Practices in the University System of Georgia* 3 (2021): 7–8. https://www.usg.edu/facultydevelopment/assets/facultydevelopment/documents/ebook/swan.pdf.

[5] Communicating expectations and explaining the steps that need to be undertaken in discipline-based research promotes student success and inclusivity, as discussed in Amanda L. Folk, "Reframing information literacy as academic cultural capital: A critical and equity-based foundation for practice, assessment, and scholarship," *College & Research Libraries* 80, no. 5 (2019): 658–673.

which is known as garum—so that I could share my progress on that topic with the class; my in-process materials were also posted as models for student submissions. So, for example, once topics have been assigned, I planned to talk to the students about how *The World of Pompeii* suggests several ways in which one could approach the topic of garum and its presence in the material record of Pompeii: its role in the larger economy, where it appears in shops; how and where it was made; or how it fits into their gastronomical culture, where I could look at kitchens in public and residential contexts. I could bring *The World of Pompeii* into class and show them how this text provides supporting bibliography for each of those approaches as well as a handy glossary of terms to demonstrate why I recommend this source as the one that all students should use to start their research. Then, I could go onto the classroom computer and show them how I would find the cited bibliography in our library or, for those sources not in our library, how I would place an interlibrary loan to have these materials sent to me. While all of this information would also be also posted on our learning management system so that students could access it outside of class, I know that finding accessible sources is often challenging for my students, who have never before undertaken specialized research in ancient art. At our institution, we also have the possibility of holding a class meeting in a library computer lab, which allows students place interlibrary loan orders as they sit at a computer while being overseen by a librarian as well as myself. Future student submissions, such as research summaries and annotated bibliographies, also help to ensure that students are understanding all the material they are finding.

In addition to the making sure that students will have enough accessible bibliography for their research projects, it is also important to consider how students would access the content knowledge that forms the basis of the information that I will be presenting to the class myself. Many of the text on Pompeii are either very general or very specialized and, in some instances, very expensive. I decided on two inexpensive paperback books,[6] one on the history of the city and one that focused on the houses; both are grounded in academic research, but their tone and style make them more accessible to non-specialists. I also planned on making my PowerPoint lectures available on our learning management system once they had been presented in class. As much as possible, however, I wanted to make the focus on learning through student activities that would be supplemented with textbooks and instructor presentations, although I recognized that there could certainly be more than one approach or even a blending of approaches employed to meet this goal. I reflected on how I might scaffold student learning in these activities to allow for a progression of

---

[6] For those specifically interested in this topic, know that I use Paul Zanker, *Pompeii: Public and Private Life* (Cambridge, Massachusetts: Harvard University Press, 1999) and Andrew Wallace-Hadrill, *Houses and Society in Pompeii and Herculaneum* (Princeton, New Jersey: Princeton University Press, 1996).

increasingly complicated engagements with content.[7] I felt like the multifaceted content associated with the Roman house was an excellent topic around which activities could be designed, but I wanted to introduce students to the public buildings of Pompeii first. I also wanted to make sure that students became accustomed to communicating with one another and engaging in self-directed activities from the first day of class. The rest of the discussion explains the content and activities I designed to meet all the course goals I envisioned.

The first activity I designed was a variation on the standard "class introduction" activity. I began class by asking the class what would think of our university if we found it buried in ash thousands of years from today. They will start to notice that many of the large buildings on the map do not appear to be academic and are instead associated with student living and athletics. Then I start to question if future archeologist will understand these spaces the same way we do and pushed them to consider what surviving features and objects would allow for the categorization into different spaces. This usually leads to some interesting reinterpretations, where students try and imagine areas they know well with a different perspective; one of my favorite interpretations came when several students decided that our campus would have looked like a religious cult that worshiped our mascot. After that class discussion, I break the class into pairs and have each student describe a personal space and the material culture that occupies it to another student. Then, each student introduces the other student to the class on their analysis of the object and environment that was described to them. This introduction activity always gets the class talking and, often, laughing together. This is an important goal, as not only will many of the course activities involve group work, but the student-based content of the final makes students stakeholders in each other's success, so students will need to work collaboratively to transform the classroom into an effective research community.

The content for the first week of class is on the destruction and rediscovery of Pompeii. I start with an explanation of the different physical processes that both destroyed and preserved elements from Pompeii. Then, we start to discuss the rediscovery of Pompeii in the eighteenth century and how the site influenced arts and culture of that time. I expose them to the widely held notion that Pompeii was a place "frozen in time" at the moment of its destruction. I break students into groups and provide each group with an example of art, architecture, furniture, movie poster, or song inspired by Pompeii and ask students to discuss how that object relates to the "idea" of Pompeii in later times and places. Students quickly come to understand that rather than undertaking in romantic imaginations associated with Pompeii's final days, the goal of the course is to try and restore real life back to Pompeii. Also, rather than seeing the site as eternally preserved, we will study the many changes that

---

[7] Krista D. Glazewski and Cindy E. Hmelo-Silver, "Scaffolding and supporting use of information for ambitious learning practices," *Information and Learning Sciences* 120, no. 1/2 (2019): 39–58.

impacted the town from its founding to its destruction. This activity makes the transition to the unit on the history of Pompeii seem like a natural next step, but it is particularly critical to keep this focus on ongoing transformation in the following unit on domestic homes, as such elements of change are much less obvious to students than when analyzing public monuments. Also, it is critically important to keep this element of change in mind with the actual presentation of material to students. Employing a variety of instructional methods not only promotes student engagement, but also creates a more inclusive learning environment that results in more effective academic performance by more students.[8]

So, when the class engages with floor plan of the Roman house, I certainly begin with the idealized model of room types described by the ancient author Vitruvius—especially as it is what I will use for the house plan on the assessment—but then I introduce lots of theories and information that both enrich and challenge that model. I use archeological reports to discuss the types of material remains found in the excavation of different rooms to show that while room labeling can often be helpful, it should not be proscriptive. I will also show students an unlabeled and empty modern house plan to show them how difficult it can be to determine the functions of room when the furnishings and décor are lacking. Indeed, I employ theoretical models drawn from anthropological studies to I encourage students to focus their analysis on the social uses of these spaces. I remind them to be mindful of how the structuring of spaces would have changed over time, both at a micro level (i.e., over the course of the day in different seasons) and at a macro level (i.e., the larger social and political changes in Roman history). I again compare the use of houses in Pompeii to modern houses, where people will often change the purpose of a room to meet their needs, such as converting a dining room into an office. This latter example is also important, as the Roman house had a much stronger public focus and was not viewed as being private in the same way as modern houses because the Roman house was place for business and social display that maintain one's status.

The flexibility of these spaces is reinforced with a class activity that engages students directly with some of the material remains that have been found in the specific rooms of certain Pompeian houses. The students work in groups to look at a provided house plan and identify the apparent function of the some of the rooms in the house. Then, the groups look at the archeological remains that were actually found in those rooms of their assigned house and discuss how that knowledge of material culture impacted their interpretation of the room.[9] The groups then present to the rest of the class some of what they

---

[8] Afzal Sayed Munna and Md Abul Kalam, "Teaching and learning process to enhance teaching effectiveness: a literature review," *International Journal of Humanities and Innovation* 4, no. 1 (2021): 1–4.

[9] Penelope M. Allison, *Pompeian Households: An Analysis of Material Culture* (Los Angeles: Cotsen Institute of Archaeology Press), https://escholarship.org/uc/item/8gp5c2nc, which includes an online compendium at https://web.archive.org/web/20190619221951/http://www.stoa.org/projects/ph/home.

discovered, which must include one room that reinforced their room classification and one room that appeared to challenge their classification. Once all groups have presented, we then reflect on some of the potential challenges to our interpretation of the finds, such as objects that may have fallen in from upper stories, changes in room use during the eruption, and post-eruption disturbance. This activity is a more active challenge to the interpretation of Pompeii as a city "frozen in time," aspects of which are often presented by students as part of their own presentations even before our concluding class discussion.

After all of this information on the structure of the house has been presented and discussed, I break students into groups and ask them to design their own floor plan for an ancient Roman house in the blank templates provided. Students are asked to create the best lines of sight along with most effective movement through the house as possible in order to make the house appear as impressive as it can to visitors. This task is complicated by the irregular spaces and varieties in size that characterize the provided floor plans. These floor plans, however, are taken from the real plots of ancient houses at Pompeii and immediately reveal the differences between the "real" and "ideal" spaces of Roman houses. Moreover, because more than one group is given the same floor plan, the resulting presentations are an excellent way to explore different solutions to a problem as well as evaluate the strengths and weakness of each choice. In this way, my non-specialist students are starting to grapple with some of the same larger issues that I have addressed within my own professional scholarship. However, the organization and movement through the house is not limited only to architectural choices. Students are also asked how they could design the décor—mainly through wall-painting, mosaics, small statuary, and some limited items of furniture—to influence one's experience of the house. This allows students to understand how ancient Pompeian décor was also deigned with function in mind, including helping to direct a visitor's passage through the house.

However, this problem-based learning activity that asks students to design an effective floorplan for the irregular shape provided is not the only way that students engage with the functional and social space of the Roman house. In order to enliven these ancient spaces and generate more student engagement, I start this next phase of study by engaging in some role-playing. I transform myself into a "Century 1" Real-Estate Trainer and tell students they will need to employ persuasive writing and speaking to sell houses and earn their "Pompeian red" realtor blazers. I give students realtor tours of existing houses at Pompeii—which include the ones they are required to know for the assessment—explaining useful features and pointing out how less effective design were deemphasized by the selected style of Roman wall-painting as well as other aspects of the décor. Students are then assigned their own house to sell—which were taken from the small houses depicted and described in the appendix of their required textbook on houses—then asked to write up a real-estate summary for the house and craft a sales presentation for the house. In their summary, students were required to apply the architectural knowledge of the Roman house that they learned in my "Training Presentations" and in their "Training Manual" (i.e., the textbook). In their own presentations to the Century 1 Trainer and other Trainees—which were supported by a written "realtor summary"—students were asked how they might advertise the house to potential buyers; there were told to emphasize positive aspects of the décor of the house, including applying their knowledge of the different styles of Roman wall-painting and suggesting how customers might use particular rooms in the house. Then, because multiple students were assigned to sell the same house, I have the class vote as to who sold it best in each group and explain why; this gamification technique not only gets students more closely involved in their peers' presentation, but also helps them to envision different uses for the same space, which reflects the real lack of single-use spaces in ancient Roman homes.

As I have mentioned, this course is very popular among students, who also rate the course very highly in the student opinions of instruction that are given at the end of the semester. However, I am even more pleased to report that student interest in the course also seems to correlate with student learning, as their performance on these activities is regularly above average in a course that requires extensive research, presenting, and writing about art. For example, student observations about both the physical and the social structure of the house for the realtor summaries were correct, clear, and well-supported, even though most students wrote in a light tone that mimicked the persona I adopted as their real estate trainer; what mattered most was students were using modern real estate vocabulary aptly and appropriately to provide insight into these ancient cultural spaces. I will admit that such connections with the present are an area where I also regularly learn from students, who are much more up to date on the latest trends than I am. For example, during one student's research topic on graffiti, he characterized the many comments written on the wall about the poor quality found in association with that inn's food and/or lodging as being similar to "Yelp Reviews." It is important to build up students' confidence about finding their own ways to engage with this ancient material. Indeed, I will often share with students how their lack of specialist knowledge in the topic can sometimes even be an advantage, as they are much less attached to the traditional ideas embedded in the scholarship that may need to be reassessed.

The following is a summary of my approach to designing Roman Life in Pompeii, all of which have been specifically cited by students in the student opinions of instruction at the end of the semester as a strength of the instructor or topic.

- Find an appropriate topic, being sure to consider potentially fruitful comparisons to contemporary life:

  - "I liked learning how the Pompeiians lived. Seeing how they lived compared to life today was definitely very different, but it was interesting to see the differences."

- Make sure topic is supported by many accessible resources:

  - "Strengths were the explanations, availability and complete willingness to help with any questions and vast knowledge on all topics within the range of the class."

- Tailor your approach to the topic so that non-specialists can meaningfully engage with it:

  - "Professor Swan's approach to ancient Pompeii made it easy to comprehend the course material. I gained a new perspective about Pompeii and its citizens."

- Break larger concepts down into smaller presentations and activities that build on one another:

  - "She structures the course in such a way that each activity bleeds into the other. This helps drill home what is really important and relates all aspects of the course."

- Explore concepts in a variety of ways, using as many active learning as possible:

  - "The best feature was how engaging the class was and the techniques used, like during the real estate project."

GREEK MYTHOLOGY IN ART

My Roman Life in Pompeii course is not the only place where I employ active learning and student presentation of content. My upper-division course on Greek Mythology in Art employs student activities to support pre-planned course content,[10] but it also asks students to design their own research projects. This allows for the expansion of the course content into material of the students' own choosing. Once again, the goal of the course is not focused on creating specialists in the study of specific works of Greek art, but how Greek mythology has been adapted to meet cultural needs. Students gain an appreciation of not simply how art changes over time, but why. The close iconographic study of images also shows how visual communication can be adapted to meet

---

[10] The required course textbook is Thomas Carpenter, *Art and Myth in Ancient Greece* (London: Thames & Hudson, 2021).

specific functions. Finally, Greek mythology is revealed to have concepts and themes that are still of interest to contemporary life.

On the first day of class, I have the students introduce themselves to one another with their name and one of the following: a common item (i.e., attribute) that they have with them most of the time, a place they can typically be found (context), or a thing they would normally be doing (roles). Afterward, I have an activity that asks them to introduce a Greek god to the class. Students are assigned a god and asked to research the god's origins, names, roles, attributes, and typical mythological contexts, as well as a visual analysis of an image from the textbook of their choosing that includes a depiction of their god. Students are only permitted to use peer-reviewed academic sources,[11] which are available through library reserve, and online academic databases;[12] this makes sure that the content students are creating is correct as well as appropriately supported. After students make their presentations, their PowerPoints are posted on our learning management system so that they are accessible to the entire class. These student-made materials become useful and handy references, helping everyone in the class to develop the critical iconographic skills that are essential to the effective analysis of depictions of Greek myth. While application of this knowledge will be assessed all semester by the unknown images included on every exam in the course, I also made sure to design a question for the first exam that explicitly focused on student acquisition of this foundational knowledge—asking students to directly list gods, roles, attributes, and an example of mythical context—so that students both immediately and directly how valuable their contributions were to the course.

I also have an activity where students compare and contrast a myth on an ancient Greek vase to an ancient text that recounts the same myth depicted in the vase. I then curate the images to select images depicted on ceramic vessels that are typically associated with a particular function—such as wine drinking, weddings, funerary rites, and so on—so that students can see how a vase painter will often make changes within a myth to make it more meaningful within the context associated with each vase's function. I also carefully select a text to associate with each vase that has some similarities with the image but at least one significant difference. This activity teaches students how texts can help to inform the study of ancient art while highlighting the significant differences between visual and textual narration. These utilitarian ceramic vessels also provide vivid illustrations as to how artisans can adapt the myth to a concept outside the narrative of the text. This is an important concept, as the written word is frequently given primacy over the images in educational setting, but this activity shows students the power of images and how they are effectively integrated into the daily visual culture of a society. The meaningless sequences of

---

[11] Most of the information students need can be found in Timothy Gantz, *Early Greek Myth: A Guide to Literary and Artistic Sources* (Baltimore: The Johns Hopkins University, 1996).

[12] Such as the Classical Art Research Centre (https://www.beazley.ox.ac.uk/carc) or the Perseus Digital Library (http://www.perseus.tufts.edu).

letters that appear on many Greek vases also helps to challenge notions regarding the authority of written texts, as these "nonsense inscriptions" are a visible expression of the boundaries of literacy in ancient Greece.[13]

Another activity asks students to grapple with the academic debates surrounding the identifications of some unusual scenes of myth. However, before students engage in this activity, I try and destabilize the notion that there is always an established or canonical version of a particular Greek myth. We start by discussing some approachable articles that question the traditional depictions or interpretations of myth.[14] Next I try to make analogies between the use of myth in ancient Greece and the social narratives used in postmodern society by engaging the class in some short in-class exercises. Students are asked to create stories in response to stock photos, revealing some of the themes and issues common to our culture. I also ask students to find memes that effectively alter a well-known image, character, or story, which not only suggests the absence of authorial authority, but also shows how these materials can be adapted into different contexts, so of which also alter the meaning quite dramatically. Then, in the activity itself that uses texts and images from Greek art, students are asked to evaluate the various arguments regarding the interpretation of the scene, reach a consensus on the most persuasive explanation, and then present their findings to the rest of the class. Students work on this project in groups, but two different groups work on the same scene of myth; if the two groups agree, it provides insight into how scholastic consensus is formed, but if the two groups don't agree, it shows how multivalent interpretations can often provide greater insight into the workings of visual culture than a single answer.

The course also has a semester-long research project that asks students to explore the motivation behind the use of mythological imagery in the visual arts of ancient Greece as well as in a post-Classical image that references the same myth. Students are required to prepare a research paper, presentation, and written summary for peers, as the two images selected by students will be required slides for the final exam. Not only our learning management system contained a wealth of support materials for students working on this project—such as research assistance, academic writing information, suggested paper structure, and rubrics for all materials—but there are also required research check-ins of various types of preparatory research and writing materials. These materials are assessed only in regard to the time of submission and the meeting of direction requirements, as their purpose is to help students manage their time as well as provide opportunities for feedback, usually from me, although occasionally from their peers. In the last two offerings of the course, however,

---

[13] For more information about these writings and reflections on how they may have functioned in ancient Greek society, see Sara Chiarini, *The So-called Nonsense Inscriptions on Ancient Greek Vases: Between Paideia and Paidiá* (Boston: Brill, 2018).

[14] I have had a lot of success using Gloria Ferrari, "Myth and Genre on Athenian Vases," *Classical Antiquity* 22, no. 1 (2003): 37–54 and Lorna Hardwick, "Ancient Amazons - Heroes, Outsiders or Women?" *Greece & Rome* 37, no. 1 (1990): 14–36.

I noticed that the complexity of the topic led a number of students to struggle with issues of organization in the paper. So, using the recommended format for the paper structure that I had created as a resource for students as a guide, I broke those suggestions down into specific prompts and asked the students to provide bullet point responses along with citational support. I titled this new research submission a "Responsive Outline" because I wanted students to understand that the work that they were doing for this research check-in should be an invaluable foundation for the organization of their paper. Because this is a new activity, I've only been able to employ it in a single course offering, but it appears as though it positively impacted paper structure and was also specifically cited in the student opinions of instruction as being helpful by individual students.

Below is bulleted listing of some active learning strategies that have been essential to the success of these courses, although they certainly apply outside of that context as well:

- Engage the students with some sort of activity as early as possible so that they become accustomed to active learning in the classroom.
- Design with accessible support materials in mind, being sure to pre-plan access to resources that students will need to understand the course material without prior knowledge.
- Make the students significant contributors to class content and utilize their input.
- Plan for ways to give both formative and summative feedback.
- Create additional course support materials or activities when a number of students appear to be having difficulty with the same issue.
- Design activities that challenge commonly held beliefs about course content or reflect scholarly debates to promote flexible as well as critical thinking.
- Promote the idea of multiple interpretations supported by reliable evidence and persuasive argument.
- Link past outlooks and approaches with contemporary practices whenever possible.

World Myth in Art

While both Roman Life in Pompeii and Greek Mythology in Art were taught to non-specialists, pre-requisites for the course assured that these courses would not be populated by first-year students or with majors outside of art unless there was special permission from the instructor. This is not the case for my general education course on World Mythology in Art. Knowing that mythology was a popular topic in a variety of contemporary media,[15] I wanted to capitalize on this popular interest to attract a wide variety of students using

[15] See, for example, the discussion of Joanna Paul, "The Half-Blood Hero: Percy Jackson and Mythmaking in the Twenty-First Century," in *A Handbook to the Reception of Classical Mythology*, eds. Vanda Zajko and Helena Hoyle (Hoboken, NJ: John Wiley, 2017), 229–242.

both mythology and images to engage them more meaningfully about the cultures of the past as well as the larger themes and issues that transcend these original contexts. I envisioned units that started with a specific focus on each culture but then focused on larger ideas that could be explored in connection with either other cultures and/or modern media. For example, I imagined taking a selective and focused look into African myth and art, which has not only some potent connections with others in regard to its culture practices, such as the masked dance, but also many thematic connections, such as the idea of the cosmic egg; then, I wanted to conclude the unit on Africa with an investigation into zombies, beginning with their original Haitian context and then ending within the context of later Western media.

Because I wanted students from all over campus reflect thoughtfully and meaningfully about a variety of cultures from the past as well as how they relate to the present, I decided to design this course to meet the goals for a Perspectives course. Perspective courses are a required category within my university's general education curriculum that are designed to foster interdisciplinary learning and global awareness. There are additional subcategories proscribed within Perspectives courses to highlight specific issues, and I selected the focus on "cross-cultural understanding and expression" for my course. The specific learning objectives I established were for students to recognize the variety of cultural expression found within and among global cultures, demonstrate an understanding of cross-cultural perspectives in the art and literature of different societies from the past as well as the present, and analyze visual and textual materials to make conjectures that are supported by both visual and written evidence. For the course description, which would be seen by students considering the course, I employed a more conversational tone: "What are myths and why have artists used them so frequently as the subject matter for art? This course will examine visual images of myth from around the world, exploring cultures of the past and present. We will look for points of commonality and difference in an attempt to understand how depictions of myth relate to the experience and values of each culture and period studied as well as how and why they continue to remain relevant today."

Because students were not required to have any prior knowledge of either myth or art, it was important that I design a course that effectively facilitated student engagement with the content, particularly in terms of supporting materials and activities, and assessed students appropriately. The start of the course would focus on the approach to analyzing art, particularly in terms of mythology relationship to material culture. I employed many of the approaches to analyzing art discussed in previous chapters, helping students to understand that images employed their own language that was separate—and not inferior—to written narratives. Textbook selection was critical, as most books on mythology focus on the literature and, while they often include images, these images are more commonly from cultures after the time of the original texts and are rarely subject to meaningful analysis. I decided upon Roy Willis' *World*

Mythology: The Illustrated Guide[16] because it was organized by culture, contained ancient images of myth from each culture along with visual and textual support, and had an introductory chapter that highlighted connections between works in different chapters by theme; while the text was sometimes poor in discussing the function of presented works, this weakness was something I felt I could compensate for by creating my own supporting materials and posting them on the learning management system.

In addition to being able to recognize the name, roles, and narrative context for selected mythical figures, I wanted to assess students' ability to identify the style, subject, significant visual elements, and function of selected images from past cultures. To meet all of these goals, I selected certain images from the textbook as required for the exam and promoted a study method that stressed an image-based notecard strategy that directed students to associate the culture, myth, significant figures and role, important artistic elements, and function with each required image.[17] I decided that students did not need to know the dates of individual images, as controlling that type of detailed information might distract students from the primary manner in which the course was utilizing those images. Students were assessed on exams using multiple-choice questions, some of which included images and some of which did not.[18] For example, in questions with images, I might display an image of a required slide from Egyptian culture with an arrow pointing to a mummified king in the underworld and asks students to identify that figure by name. In non-image questions, I could simply ask which god was the ruler of the dead without displaying any image; of course, although I would only ask this question if there was a required image associated with that figure and role. Creating links between images and relevant mythological content was not simply a sensible study approach for the course content, but it was also an effective learning approach more generally, as the connection of words with images has been proven to be more effective in increasing the brain's ability to recall both.[19]

It was also critical in this course for students to make connections between similar approaches to myth across cultures, which was further supported by a chapter dedicated to this topic in the textbook. For this reason, I instructed students to associate each image with themes and/or images from other cultures we studied in their study. This thematic knowledge was assessed on exams

---

[16] Roy Willis ed., *World Mythology: The Illustrated Guide* (Oxford: Oxford University Press, 2006).

[17] This study approach was also supported by a notecard activity that I discuss in greater detail in another chapter.

[18] While it is common in my discipline to include images on exams, studies have suggested the benefit of this practice outside of the arts; see Marlit A. Lindner, Johannes Schult, and Richard E. Mayer, "A multimedia effect for multiple-choice and constructed-response test items," *Journal of Educational Psychology* 114, vol. 1 (2020): 72–88.

[19] There is extensive scholarship on this subject, but it remains important to understand that the link between content and image needs to be—or be made to be—relevant to the content in order positively impact mental recall; for more on this, see Sascha Schneider et al., "The retrieval-enhancing effects of decorative pictures as memory cues in multimedia learning videos and subsequent performance tests," *Journal of Educational Psychology* 112, no. 6 (2020): 1111–1127.

using questions without images that focused on having them make effective thematic connections. For example, a theme question might ask students to correctly associate more than one mythical figure in a work connected with a notion of existence after death, which would include Osiris, but could also include Hades from Greek mythology. These types of questions increased with every exam and, unlike the rest of the exam, the content of these type of questions was cumulative over the course of the semester. This aspect encouraged students to keep looking back at older material even as we moved forward; for example, in our class discussion of zombies in Haitian art, one student noted how the zombies were always dressed in white; when another student replied that it recalled the white mummification wrappings of Osiris, it lead to a fruitful discussion of white as a common funereal color in African culture and, thus, a natural visual expression for zombies, who no longer had their soul to make them truly living beings.

Activities are an essential element to this course, not simply for enforcing and enriching this knowledge, but having students practice visual analysis as well as relating the content of the past with contemporary images, as neither of these aspects is a specific focus on the exam. While some activities may focus directly on the skill of looking closely and making inferences from supporting texts, the citation of visual evidence is an aspect of every activity. For example, in addition to having students read an article about the visual depiction of zombies in different times and cultures,[20] I also have them participate in a discussion board about depictions of zombies in modern media where students engage in some surprisingly direct discussions about race, violence, consumerism, and other contemporary issues of concern while using specific images— from the article or the web—to support their points. So, when planning my syllabus, I made sure to include time when students could make connections between mythical images from the past and the present to help students to see that not only mythmaking is alive and well today, but sometimes modern culture still grapples with some of the concerns. Regarding the conception of zombies, class conversation ultimately revolves around who holds power in a society and how power impacts concepts of otherness.

In terms of course assessment, I strive to make sure that different activities are assessed at a value appropriate to the level of time and engagement required. So, in the case of the discussion board mentioned earlier, I would make that a specific grade item worth around 5% of the course grade. A detailed visual analysis of an image in connection with a text, such as the Noah's Ark activity mentioned in a previous chapter, would be assigned as a written essay and this individual assignment and would be worth around 10% of the course grade. However, I also employ regular participation activities that are only evaluated in terms of meeting requirements and on-time submission, but which are invaluable for creating more opportunities for engagement as well as rewarding

---

[20] Elizabeth McAlister, "Slaves, Cannibals, and Infected Hyper-Whites: The Race and Religion of Zombies," *Anthropological Quarterly* 85, No. 2 (Spring 2012): 457–486.

students who regularly participate; these many activities are factored into a larger attendance and participation grade, which typically represents 15% or 20% of the total course grade. There is no rule as to what can constitute a participation activity, so they can be more formal and pre-planned activities posted on the class management system or much more spontaneous and informal calls for participation. The weekly notecard activity I describe in a later chapter would be an example of the former, so allow me to describe an example of the latter, such as calling for students to bring in an example of an archetypical hero for the class period after our discussion of that topic; rather than see it as a burden, students are often excited to explain how their favorite hero—often from video games, anime, or movies—has many of the same traits that we discussed. Small moments like these often have a significant impact, making students look at old images and texts with a new eye because they start to seem more relatable to their own experiences.

Setting up a significant portion of the course with frequent, non-numerical assessments requires regular feedback and monitoring. First, the students need to be aware of their standing; so, every week, I post each student's absences and activities on the course management system as narrative feedback within the gradebook in association with their attendance and participation grade. I also employ the learning management system to post timed announcements and email non-submitters for activity deadlines. When a student seems to be starting a pattern of absences and/or lack of participation, I email the student; note that this may also be something that your learning management system may even be able to automate. If the pattern continues after this contact, I post an alert in our university mentoring/advising portal. If this does not resolve the issue, I will ask the student to set up a meeting with me; I will email both the student and the advisor, but I will also approach the student before or after class if they are attending. Many of these interventions required only minor course accommodations or a few individual learning-support meetings; sometimes, it was simply a matter of directing students to material that was already available to them through the learning management system. However, some of these interventions identified more significant issues that were interfering in the student's learning in all their courses that semester; the latter cases are a reminder of how surprisingly easy it can be for students in larger lower-division courses to struggle without ever engaging the support-system of the university. Such outreach represents a clear investment of faculty time—and has increased dramatically since COVID[21]—but actions like these, which strengthen the relationship between instructors and students, can lead to more student academic

---

[21] The COVID pandemic clearly had a direct and immediate impact on instructors, but students proved to have more difficulties coping, which results in another secondary impact of COVID on faculty; see Jacqueline A. Goldman and Stephanie C. Bell, "Student and Faculty Coping and Impacts on Academic Success in Response to COVID-19," *Journal of Interdisciplinary Studies in Education* 11, no. 1 (2022): 74–91. Of course, the impact of all these changes needs to be carefully considered in terms of faculty members' evaluation and professional development, especially because not all faculty have been impacted equally; see Shelda Debowski, "Shifting sands: navigating being academic in an evolving sector," *Higher Education Research & Development* 41, no. 1 (2022): 7–20.

success as well as better student attitudes toward their learning;[22] it could even prove lifesaving for some students.[23] Helping students to get needed assistance to overcome the obstacles they were facing have proven to be some of the most memorable moments in my teaching career.

Generalizing from my own personal experience, below are some tips for setting up a specialized course focused on material culture of the past for general education students:

- Choose an effective topic:

    - Reflect on an aspect of your scholarship that excites you.
    - Imagine how you might introduce non-specialists to the subjects, themes, and issues associated with that scholarship.
    - Consider how the physicality of material culture might provide an accessible way for students to engage with less tangible ideas.
    - Craft a title and course description with the goal of attracting students to the course.

- Consider how students might interact appropriately with the topic:

    - Think carefully about what content students need to control and what content they simply need to know how to access.
    - Provide students with a variety of ways to engage with the material and assess those engagements in a manner that reflects the effort required for each.
    - Ask students to employ multiple skills during the process of activities.
    - Find ways to allow for the material to stand on its own as well as interrelate.

- Appreciate how many students could face challenges and plan for ways to support them:

    - Provide effective primary as well as secondary forms of content support for students.

---

[22] There are many studies that show how the student perception instructor care improves student academic performance and attitude toward the instructor, but particularly for students in crisis, discussed by Mariana T. Guzzardo et al., "'The Ones that Care Make all the Difference': Perspectives on Student-Faculty Relationships," *Innovative Higher Education* 46, no. 1 (2021): 41–58.

[23] Instructor training in identifying students at risk for suicide has been shown to increase instructor knowledge and confidence in handling these situations; see Ashley L. Sylvara and Jon T. Mandracchia, "An investigation of gatekeeper training and self efficacy for suicide intervention among college/university faculty," *Crisis* 43, vol. 3 (2019): 383–389, https://doi.org/10.1027/0227-5910/a000577.

- Make expectations for assessments and activities clear through exam guides, suggested study approaches, clear and detailed directions, rubrics, and/or examples.
- Post different types of resource support on the learning management system for everyone, but also make specific recommendations to students individually as needed.
- Allot time every week to posting feedback and monitoring student performance.
- Employ the resources of the university to identify concerns before the student has reached a point where it would be problematic to correct and recover.

REFERENCES

Allison, Penelope M. *Pompeian Households: An Analysis of Material Culture* (Los Angeles, CA: Cotsen Institute of Archaeology Press, 2004).

Alomari, Islam, Hosam Al-Samarraie, and Reem Yousef. "The Role of Gamification Techniques in Promoting Student Learning: A Review and Synthesis." *Journal of Information Technology Education: Research* 18 (2019): 395–417.

Carpenter, Thomas. *Art and Myth in Ancient Greece* (London: Thames & Hudson, 2021).

Chiarini, Sara. *The So-called Nonsense Inscriptions on Ancient Greek Vases: Between Paideia and Paidiá* (Boston: Brill, 2018).

Debowski, Shelda. "Shifting Sands: Navigating Being Academic in an Evolving Sector." *Higher Education Research & Development* 41, no. 1 (2022): 7–20.

Dobbins, J. and Pedar W. Foss, eds. *The World of Pompeii* (New York: Routledge, 2007).

Ferrari, Gloria. "Myth and Genre on Athenian Vases." *Classical Antiquity* 22, no. 1 (2003): 37–54.

Folk, Amanda L. "Reframing Information Literacy as Academic Cultural Capital: A Critical and Equity-based Foundation for Practice, Assessment, and Scholarship." *College & Research Libraries* 80, no. 5 (2019): 658–673.

Gantz, Timothy. *Early Greek Myth: A Guide to Literary and Artistic Sources* (Baltimore, MD: The Johns Hopkins University, 1996).

Glazewski, Krista D. and Cindy E. Hmelo-Silver. "Scaffolding and Supporting Use of Information for Ambitious Learning Practices." *Information and Learning Sciences* 120, no. 1/2 (2019): 39–58.

Goldman, Jacqueline A. and Stephanie C. Bell. "Student and Faculty Coping and Impacts on Academic Success in Response to COVID-19." *Journal of Interdisciplinary Studies in Education* 11, no. 1 (2022): 74–91.

Guzzardo, Mariana T., Nidhi Khosla, Annis Lee Adams, Jeffra D. Bussmann, Alina Engelman, Natalie Ingraham, Ryan Gamba, Ali Jones-Bey, Matthew D. Moore, Negin R. Toosi, and Sarah Taylor. "'The Ones That Care Make all the Difference': Perspectives on Student-Faculty Relationships." *Innovative Higher Education* 46, no. 1 (2021): 41–58.

Hardwick, Lorna. "Ancient Amazons - Heroes, Outsiders or Women?" *Greece & Rome* 37, no. 1 (1990): 14–36.

Hafeez, Muhammad. "Systematic Review on Modern Learning Approaches, Critical Thinking Skills and Students Learning Outcomes." *Indonesian Journal of Educational Research and Review* 4, no. 1 (2021): 167–178.

Lindner, Marlit A., Johannes Schult, and Richard E. Mayer. "A Multimedia Effect for Multiple-Choice and Constructed-Response Test Items." *Journal of Educational Psychology* 114, no. 1 (2020): 72–88.

McAlister, Elizabeth. "Slaves, Cannibals, and Infected Hyper-Whites: The Race and Religion of Zombies." *Anthropological Quarterly* 85, no. 2 (Spring 2012): 457–486.

Munna, Afzal Sayed and Md Abul Kalam. "Teaching and Learning Process to Enhance Teaching Effectiveness: A Literature Review." *International Journal of Humanities and Innovation* 4, no. 1 (2021): 1–4.

Paul, Joanna. "The Half-Blood Hero: Percy Jackson and Mythmaking in the Twenty-First Century." In *A Handbook to the Reception of Classical Mythology*. Edited by Vanda Zajko and Helena Hoyle, 229–242 (Hoboken, NJ: John Wiley, 2017).

Schneider, Sascha, Steve Nebel, Maik Beege, and Günter Daniel Rey. "The Retrieval-Enhancing Effects of Decorative Pictures as Memory Cues in Multimedia Learning Videos and Subsequent Performance Tests." *Journal of Educational Psychology* 112, no. 6 (2020): 1111–1127.

Swan, Glenda. "Integrating Student Research into Course Content." *Engaged Student Learning: Essays on Best Practices in the University System of Georgia* 3 (2021): 7–8. https://www.usg.edu/facultydevelopment/assets/facultydevelopment/documents/ebook/swan.pdf.

Sylvara, Ashley L. and Jon T. Mandracchia. "An Investigation of Gatekeeper Training and Self-Efficacy for Suicide Intervention Among College/University Faculty." *Crisis* 43, no. 3 (2019): 383–389. https://doi.org/10.1027/0227-5910/a000577.

Wallace-Hadrill, Andrew. *Houses and Society in Pompeii and Herculaneum* (Princeton, NJ: Princeton University Press, 1996).

Willis, Roy, ed. *World Mythology: The Illustrated Guide* (Oxford: Oxford University Press, 2006).

Zanker, Paul. *Pompeii: Public and Private Life* (Cambridge, MA: Harvard University Press, 1999).

CHAPTER 5

Letting Students Shape the Future

Contemporary students have become accustomed to having a high degree of choice; indeed, the most recent generation of students is often characterized to as being accustomed to an "on demand" lifestyle.[1] In order to attract students, higher education has certainly expanded its choices for students in regard to their physical and social experience environment on campus. However, it is important to realize that it is not simply the option of the choices that influences students, but also the manner in which those options are offered and how students engage with those choices.[2] This illustrates how the "student choice" is actual a much more complicated issue than it may first appear, particularly when one is trying to employ it effectively within the classroom setting.

Options for student choice within higher education have been more limited in regard to their academic experience than in other areas. Although the COVID emergency necessitated the creation of many types of alternative formats for learning, many of the options made available to students during that time—as well as to faculty—have since been rescinded by a number of institutions.[3] This desire to limit online learning may be explained by the fact that some online courses did not utilize very effective instructional practices for that

---

[1] Christopher S. Keator, *The Digital Era of Learning: Novel Educational Strategies and Challenges for Teaching Students in the 21st Century* (New York: Nova Science Publishers, 2021) x.

[2] A recent discussion about many of the non-objective factors influencing student choice can be found in J. S. Ravi Kumar, T. Narayana Reddy, and Syed Mohammad Ghouse, "Role of Servicescape on Student Institution Choice," *Asian Journal of Management* 12, no. 3 (2021): 271–278.

[3] This comes from my experience with my own institution, which promised a completely "normal" 2021–2022 academic year that included a format change to face to face for most of the online and hybrid courses offered the previous academic year.

© The Author(s), under exclusive license to Springer Nature Switzerland AG 2023
G. Swan, *ReEnvisioning the Material Past,*
https://doi.org/10.1007/978-3-031-24027-0_5

particular type of learning format;[4] additionally, there have been studies that suggest that virtual learning had a negative correlation with student achievement, particularly among marginalized groups.[5] Still, despite the success of some of these choice-based alternatives even before the time of COVID,[6] course format options vary greatly by institution and are more often made at an administrative level. Because most instructors are not able to allow students options regarding their choice of course format or curricular design, such aspects will not be a focus of this discussion.

Despite some of these larger limitations, there has been a movement to expand choice within the classroom in order to increase student engagement. Students' ability to have choices and/or make decisions in a course increases their feelings of empowerment along with their cognitive and behavioral engagement with course content.[7] As an instructional approach, student choice has been associated with the creation of self-directed learners.[8] Student choice is also strongly connected to other forms of engaged learning, such as problem-based learning and gamification.[9] However, simply providing more choices to students is not the solution; in fact, too many options can have a negative impact on student motivation.[10] The key to success is for the instructor to

[4] While not all students reacted positively to approaches seen as effective online practices, their use still had a more positive impact overall, as seen in Barbara Means and Julie Neisler, "Teaching and learning in the time of COVID: The student perspective." *Online Learning* 25, no. 1 (2021): 8–27. While there are many good articles about specific online learning practices designed to improve online engagement and learning, I very much appreciate the holistic and non-directive approach outlined by David Starr-Glass, "Purposefully-Designed and Mindfully-Facilitated Online Courses," in *Handbook of Research on Managing and Designing Online Courses in Synchronous and Asynchronous Environments*, eds. Gurhan Durak and Serkan Cankaya (Hershey, PA: IGI Global, 2021), 251–272.

[5] Jennifer Darling-Aduana, Sarah S. Barry, Henry T. Woodyard, and Tim R. Sass, "Learning-Mode Choice, Student Engagement, and Achievement Growth During the COVID-19 Pandemic," *EdWorkingPaper* 22-536 (February 2022): 1–43, retrieved from Annenberg Institute at Brown University, https://doi.org/10.26300/jxcj-gs73.

[6] For example, see Travis R. McDowell et al., "A Student-Choice Model to Address Diverse Needs and Promote Active Learning," *Journal of Science Education and Technology* 28 (2019): 321–328.

[7] Brett D. Jones and Devin Carter, "Relationships between students' course perceptions, engagement, and learning," *Social Psychology of Education* 22, no. 4 (2019): 819–839.

[8] Of course, there are many other factors that impact the development of self-determination skills in students, as explained in a report prepared by Christopher W. Brandt, *Measuring Student Success Skills: A Review of the Literature on Self-Directed Learning* (Dover, New Hampshire: National Center for the Improvement of Educational Assessment: 2020), https://www.nciea.org/sites/default/files/publications/CFA-SlfDirLearningLitReport-R2.pdf.

[9] Some recent discussions include Weber R. Irembere, "Fostering Creative Skills for Students Using Project-Based Learning," *International Forum Journal* 22, no. 2 (2019): 102–115 and Caitlin Hayward and Barry Fishman, "Gameful Learning: Designing with Motivation in Mind," *Interdisciplinary Society of the Learning Sciences Proceedings* 2 (2020): 1007–1014, https://doi.org/10.22318/ICLS2020.1007.

[10] Sascha Schneider, "Are there never too many choice options? The effect of increasing the number of choice options on learning with digital media," *Human Behavior and Emerging Technologies* 3, no. 5 (2021): 759–775.

select opportunities for the incorporation of a reasonable number of choices within a course that are appropriate to its design, goals, and placement within the curriculum.[11]

Images are great opportunities to allow students to exercise choice. Images, like all forms of supporting evidence, can be used to support, refute, or expand an element of research. Also, while many people often think of images as singular and unique, most are part of a much larger expression of material culture, so picking one image over another is often just a matter of personal choice because there is rarely only one "correct" image selection. For example, when I teach the High Classical period of Athenian art, I contextualize it within the Greeks expulsion of the Persians along with radical democracy in Athens that accentuated their own particular socio-political values, all of which I associate with the idealized perfectionism found in the artistic expression of the time. The mathematical perfectionism found in the *Parthenon*, the canon of idealized proportions illustrated by Polykleitos' *Spear-Bearer*, and even private monuments of the time are all equally effective examples for illustrating how the culture of that time and place manifested itself through visual expression. So, no matter which image is selected as required for my Art History Survey exam from this period, I still expect that students will not only be able to cite and discuss the required work as visual evidence about High Classical Athenian culture, but even be able to identify the High Classical style in works that they have not previously seen.[12]

Asking students to employ image images as evidentiary support in written or presented materials not only leads to greater engagement with an activity, but also appears to increase critical thinking and learning.[13] It is also very easy for students to find and incorporate images within most learning management systems, Word documents, and PowerPoints even without the use of any specialized programs. Still, while students are often already accustomed to the mechanics of finding and inserting images, they are unaccustomed to effectively selecting, analyzing, and contextualizing those images as evidence within an academic presentation or paper; similarly, many instructors fail to critically assess the use or citation of images in student work.[14] There are many types of activities that instructors can use to teach students to analyze and employ images thoughtfully, many of which have already been discussed in this text,

---

[11] For example, see the recent article discussing different schema for project-based learning courses designed engage student choice at a variety of levels by Eun Hye Son and Tara Penry, "Variations in Project-Based Course Design," *Journal of Problem Based Learning in Higher Education* (2022): 1–16, https://journals.aau.dk/index.php/pbl/article/view/6821.

[12] I also support this approach with a recommended study technique that is not limited to notecards that focus on the style, context, and meaning of individual images required for the exam, but also notecards that explore important larger aspects of the culture that include its visual expression.

[13] Mary Ann Hollingsworth, "Pictures Worth a Thousand Words: A New Approach in Graduate School," *Journal of Literature and Art Studies* 8, no. 1 (2018): 153–158.

[14] Both of these points are addressed in the article by Krystyna K. Matusiak et al., "Visual literacy in practice: Use of images in students' academic work," *College & Research Libraries* 80, no. 1 (2019): 123–139.

but this chapter discusses some more specific examples where I have incorporated the decisions and work-product of students into my courses.

Students will take images more seriously if they are assessed on them in some way. While activities, presentations, and papers are all excellent options, consider incorporating images into exams and/or asking students to employ images in connection with study preparation. In my general education courses, activities that require students to go on our learning management and make a post that uses words as well as image(s) to summarize a specific example of course content have proven to be effective reviews. The content of these student post can be limited to a chapter or class meeting, or it can be a required definition or concept for an upcoming exam. In the case of activities tied to exams, I require that student posts use the same format as the study method I have already been promoting and modeling to further reinforce what I know to be an effective approach to learning course content. Also, because these activities are shared, they make the preparation of those study aids easier for all the students in the course. While my own courses are based in the arts, aspects of these approach should still prove effective for many other disciplines.[15]

For example, in my Introduction to Visual Arts course, I have asked students to select a term or concept from the study guide for the first exam on the elements and principles of design and then post a notecard on that selected term or concept. This notecard was to be supported with a variety of visual and written evidence. It needed to recount the textbook's definition of the selected term or concept as well as a characterization of the term or concept in simple, everyday language. It should also include a fine art image from the textbook along with a brief explanation as to how the image illustrated the selected term or concept. Finally, the notecard needed to contain a photo of taken by the student of something other than a work of fine art with a brief explanation as to how the photo also illustrated the selected term or concept.

Of course, having students support each other's study doesn't always have to be a formal activity. While it is not uncommon for me to include specific study tips in conjunction with the presentation of course content, I often find that it is class involvement that leads to the most effective retention. So, I have begun to highlight the process of review periodically during class to have students directly reflect on their own learning and contribute to the learning of their peers. I will often take a moment in class to ask students, "So, how are we all going to remember this for the exam?" This often leads to some group brainstorming of some quick study tips and tricks for a term, concept, or process associated with the image being displayed at that moment. One of the

---

[15] There are a number of academic articles from instructors in a variety of fields who documented improvement in exam performance with the use of images, but I even discovered one who also had the students prepare those aids to learning: Christopher Bozek, "Enabling Students to Create Materials for their Language Learning Classes," in *Proceedings of the 2021 International Workshop on Modern Science and Technology* (Kitami, Japan: International Center of National University Corporation Kitami Institute of Technology, 2021), 309–312, https://kitami-it.repo.nii.ac.jp/records/2000142#.YpDfSajMLIU.

most successful examples even connected several review moments that were developed during an Introduction to Visual Arts course meeting focused on printmaking. By overexaggerating some of the hand gestures I use while speaking, the class developed kinesthetic movements to represent the different types of printmaking: raise your hands above your head and say "relief" (as the area to be printed is above the surface of the matrix), then touch your toes and say "intaglio" (as the area to be printed is below the surface of the matrix), then wave your hands at your waist and say "lithography" (as the area to be printed is on the surface of the matrix), and then bend over and pull an invisible squeegee and say "serigraphy" (as the print is made by pushing ink through a screen that is the matrix). Not only did students that semester perform much better on the printmaking questions than previous semesters, but I even noticed several student employing smaller versions of these movements while they were taking the exam.

For my Art History Survey course, I used to use student feedback during class discussion to select which images from each class period would be required images for the exam, but with the coming of COVID and its strong impact on the classroom experience, I decided to do some reverse engineering. I employed our learning management system to have students post notecards on the images from the previous week that they believed should be included on the exam, along with an argument about how each selected image reflected its original time, place, and meaning/function. Then, I just selected the most effective student posts to determine the specific material that would form the required content for the exam. This proved so successful, I not only continue to use this approach in this course, but also modified it for use in several different lower-division courses as well. Below, though, I will explain in detail how I designed and evaluated these activities in connection with my Mythology in World Art course (note that my larger design of this course was discussed in a previous chapter), as I think the larger and more thematic focus of those notecards is the most adaptable element for use in other disciplines.

Each week, an assigned notecard activity in my Mythology in World Art course asked students to select an image that was discussed in class the previous week and then post specified content about their selected image on our online learning management system. As someone whose pedagogy is solidly based in transparency in teaching, the activity directions clearly explained the value of this activity to students: "These posts will allow students to influence the selection of required images as well as allow collaboration in the 'crowd sourcing' of effective study aids." All images were accessible to students in the required textbook as well as in a posted PowerPoint; this PowerPoint was an expanded version of what was presented in class and included additional notes along with other supporting resources. The prompts for the notecard activity were based on the recommended study strategies for the material that I presented in the first couple of weeks of the course. Below I've listed the specific prompts that were provided to students, along with directions to use the image's figure number, culture, and title for the title of their post:

- Summarize the myth(s) being depicted in the selected image.
- Identify significant figures within the myth and their larger roles.
- Point out important artistic elements (attributes, symbols, etc.).
- Reflect on the function of image (if applicable).
- Connect to a larger theme:

  - Either explain how the selected image can be associated with a "Great Theme of Myth" as discussed in our textbook
  - or specifically compare the selected image to an image from another culture that we have studied with the same theme.

- Relate the myth to something you and/or your peers are more familiar with.

Not only breaking down students responses reinforced the study approach using notecards that I had already outlined for students at the start of the course, but these prompts also helped to ensure that students were more focused on analyzing the selected image and the associated myth rather than simply cutting and pasting from the textbook, PowerPoint, or an online source about the narrative or image more generally.[16] While reliable outside sources were permitted, a zero was assigned to any activity that omitted or incorrectly cited online sources. I also employed a setting within the online discussion board to make sure that students could not see the posts of other students until they made their own. I did, however, monitor posts myself so that I could provide any corrective feedback; this also allowed me to offer students the opportunity to make corrections in advance of the deadline. While I gave much more feedback in the first few weeks that the activity was instituted, students seemed to appreciate this ongoing feedback, and it had the added benefit of motivating more students not to wait until right before the deadline to make a post; later in the semester, I also employed activities that had students provide feedback to the posts of others.[17]

Once the deadline for the activity had been reached, I selected the most effectively presented images. While my learning management system has the ability for students to vote up or down the posts of others, I did not use this option because I felt that it would delay the selection of images for too long. These selected images served as the required images for our next exam, and I always made sure post them promptly after the deadline to reinforce prompt

---

[16] Having student posts generate information beyond what is presented to them is an important element to the construction of learning and also promotes greater peer interaction with posts; see Mladen Raković et al., "Fine grained analysis of students' online discussion posts," *Computers & Education* 157 (2020): 103982, https://doi.org/10.1016/j.compedu.2020.103982.

[17] For more about how both instructor and peer interaction can help student learning, see Vinothini Vasodavan, Dorothy DeWitt, Norlidah Alias, and Mariani Md Noh, "E-moderation skills in discussion forums: Patterns of online interactions for knowledge construction," *Pertanika Journal of Social Sciences and Humanities* 28, no. 4 (2020): 3025–3045.

and regular study habits. Note, however, that it was not uncommon for there to be multiple students who posted on the same image. These moments of reduplication allowed students to compare and contrast their own responses to others and see how they might improve their own study materials for this image as well as for future postings. I also offered an opportunity for students to make late submissions, but I required students posting late to select an image from the most recent update to the list of required slides. In the few instances there was some critical image that I felt had to be added even though no one posted on it, allowing late posts provided a second chance for that image to be analyzed by a student, although I always remained prepared to make my own post if needed.

The data I collected during the 2020–2021 year showed improved student academic performance on exams in comparison to previous offerings of the course. Additionally, there were more students regularly posting notecards than those who had engaged in the weekly online activities I had employed in past semesters, despite the commensurate requirements and value of these participation activities. This suggests that the potential for student work to contribute directly to course content created more incentive for students to participate. Finally, in the student evaluations given at the end of every semester, a number of students specifically cited that the weekly notecard activities had been very helpful in helping them prepare for the course exams. While I suspect that students who were absent from class because of COVID might have found the notecards a particularly valuable resource because they hadn't been able to be in class to hear the material being presented and ask questions, I was unable to isolate this variable with the data collection methods I employed.

Another aspect I appreciated about this activity came in Spring 2022, when it became evident to me as part of my regular feedback to the weekly notecards that some students were still struggling more than in past semesters to identify effective themes. In response, I came up with a new activity that asked student to craft a discussion post that identified a meaningful thematic connection between images from three different cultures while still acknowledging how that theme was specifically expressed in each image in a manner specific to the culture that created it. The selection of theme and images was left to student choice. Not only students performed well on the activity, but more students correctly answered the theme questions on following exam than the previous one. While this activity was designed and instituted because of an issue in a particular semester, it appears to have been so effective that I am considering including it as a regular part of future course offerings.

In my advanced courses, involving student-selected research into the course content is a regular occurrence. As has been discussed in previous chapters, student content becomes integrated into course content in a variety of ways, from the start to the end of the course. The more time students spend on a research project, the more ways I work to integrate it directly into course content and assessment. For this reason, the semester-long research projects that are a part of every upper-division course I teach become a significant focus of course content at the end of every course, particularly on the final exam. These research projects may be individual rather than group undertakings,[18] but they require that students invest in learning not simply from their own content, but also from the content of others. I also tell students that I use the best examples of student research when I design the final exam, which motivates some students to really excel, as they assume that they will perform much better on a question about material that they have researched in depth themselves.

Holding other students responsible for content prepared by peers requires support as well as feedback from both the instructor and students. Student content information must, of course, be available to everyone in the class. While learning management systems make this easy, some types of research benefit from being condensed and represented. For example, rather than asking the entire class to read all the research papers of their peers, consider requiring students to post a written and/or visual summary of their research on a discussion board, ideally in a manner that reinforces the recommended study technique for the associated assessment. Making this summary also helps students to take a step back and envision how their detailed investigation of their own topic can relate in a larger way to the topics researched by others. It is also useful to remind students how effective summarization is a skill that can be useful for preparing abstracts needed for many other pre-professional activities beyond the classroom, such as applications for internships, grants, graduate study applications, and employment. Still, it can be helpful to employ other activities to foster more active dialog between students about their contributions to content. I often assign each presenter a peer respondent, who is responsible for asking the first question. I have also made the presenter responsible for posting an "update" to their summary after hearing the questions asked after their presentation; these updates can clarify already posted material, add new material, or make a connection between their material and that of another presenter. For questions that come up during study, I employ a dedicated discussion board where students could post and answer questions about research topics. For the past several semesters, however, students have voluntarily instituted their own text-messaging group among themselves for this function; so, while I still employ that discussion board, I now request that any questions without a text response within 24 hours be reposted there so I can make sure that they are addressed.

Student feedback in the student opinions of instruction in my upper-division courses regularly cite the variety of ways in which they interacted with course content as a positive, as well as how I helped to facilitate that interaction; the importance of these aspects is also cited in other studies of scholarship of

---

[18] While I certainly employ group projects, they are often understood as synonymous with active learning, as seen in the discussion by David W. Johnson and Roger T. Johnson, "Cooperative Learning: The Foundation for Active Learning," in *Active Learning – Beyond the Future*, ed. Silvio Manuel Brito (London: IntechOpen, 2019), 59–70, https://directory.doabooks.org/handle/20.500.12854/40081.

teaching and learning.[19] Allowing students to select their own object of material culture to research and present, even within a proscribed topic, is an easy way to activate interest because the analysis and contextualization of an image inherently encompasses such variety of approaches and perspectives.[20] Acting as a good facilitator certainly requires equal adaptability. However, by promoting an environment of cooperative learning, instructors can admit whenever they encounter elements beyond their own knowledge and/or experience and then model for students the information and outreach that can help to correct that deficiency; paradoxically, this approach can be especially useful for instructors who are already more likely to be viewed with bias because of some aspect of their personal identity.[21] Indeed, the focus on how visual culture involves the construction of meaning helps students to become more self-aware about how they come to knowledge for themselves.[22]

References

Bozek, Christopher. "Enabling Students to Create Materials for Their Language Learning Classes." In *Proceedings of the 2021 International Workshop on Modern Science and Technology*, 309–312. (Kitami, Japan: International Center of National University Corporation Kitami Institute of Technology, 2021). https://kitami-it. repo.nii.ac.jp/records/2000142#.YpDfSajMLIU.

Brandt, Christopher W. *Measuring Student Success Skills: A Review of the Literature on Self-Directed Learning* (Dover, NH: National Center for the Improvement of Educational Assessment, 2020). https://www.nciea.org/sites/default/files/publications/CFA-SlfDirLearningLitReport-R2.pdf.

[19] Guan-Yu Lin, Yi-Shun Wang, and Yong Ni Lee, "Investigating factors affecting learning satisfaction and perceived learning in flipped classrooms: the mediating effect of interaction," *Interactive Learning Environments* (2022): 1–22. https://doi.org/10.1080/10494820.2021.2018616.

[20] Even the process of how the works of visual culture have been studied and discussed through history can be a subject of inquiry, as seen in Lindsay Persohn, "Curation as Methodology," *Qualitative Research* 21, no. 1 (2021): 20–41.

[21] I have written about my own experience about course teaching on African-American art as someone who was white as well as a non-content specialist in Glenda Swan, "Minorities' Views and Minorities Viewed: Embracing Minorities in the Classroom and Visual Culture," in *Fostering a Climate of Inclusion in the College Classroom: The Missing Voice of the Humanities* by Lavonna Lovern (Cham, Switzerland: Springer, 2018), 73–90. While there is no single path to success, presenting oneself as a fellow learner and integrating students into the interpretation and production of course content knowledge helps to build a relationship of trust and respect in the classroom; see also Jung-ah Choi, "Shared Authority and Epistemological Struggles: Tales of Three Racial Groups of Professors," *Voices of Reform: Educational Research to Inform and Reform* 4, no. 1 (2021): 10–23.

[22] This is the foundation behind Constructivist Pedagogy, which is a core element of many active learning approaches. While this approach has a record of success and there is a push by many universities for more use of this approach within courses, it still needs to be thoughtfully and carefully applied; for more, see Kate O'Connor, "Constructivism, curriculum and the knowledge question: tensions and challenges for higher education," *Studies in Higher Education* 47, vol. 2 (2022): 412–422.

Choi, Jung-ah. "Shared Authority and Epistemological Struggles: Tales of Three Racial Groups of Professors." *Voices of Reform: Educational Research to Inform and Reform* 4, no. 1 (2021): 10–23.

Darling-Aduana, Jennifer, Sarah S. Barry, Henry T. Woodyard, and Tim R. Sass. "Learning-Mode Choice, Student Engagement, and Achievement Growth During the COVID-19 Pandemic." *EdWorkingPaper* 22-536 (February 2022): 1–43. Retrieved from Annenberg Institute at Brown University. https://doi.org/10.26300/jxcj-gs73.

Hayward, Caitlin and Barry Fishman, "Gameful Learning: Designing with Motivation in Mind." *Interdisciplinary Society of the Learning Sciences Proceedings* 2 (2020): 1007–1014. https://doi.org/10.22318/icls2020.1007.

Hollingsworth, Mary Ann. "Pictures Worth a Thousand Words: A New Approach in Graduate School." *Journal of Literature and Art Studies* 8, no. 1 (2018): 153–158.

Irembere, Weber R. "Fostering Creative Skills for Students Using Project-Based Learning." *International Forum Journal* 22, no. 2 (2019) 102–115.

Jones, Brett D. and Devin Carter. "Relationships Between Students' Course Perceptions, Engagement, and Learning." *Social Psychology of Education* 22, no. 4 (2019): 819–839.

Johnson, David W. and Roger T. Johnson. "Cooperative Learning: The Foundation for Active Learning." In *Active Learning – Beyond the Future.* Edited by Silvio Manuel Brito, 59–70. (London: IntechOpen, 2019). https://directory.doabooks.org/handle/20.500.12854/40081.

Keator, Christopher S. *The Digital Era of Learning: Novel Educational Strategies and Challenges for Teaching Students in the 21st Century* (New York: Nova Science Publishers, 2021).

Kumar, J. S. Ravi T. Narayana Reddy, and Syed Mohammad Ghouse. "Role of Servicescape on Student Institution Choice." *Asian Journal of Management* 12, no. 3 (2021): 271–278.

Lin, Guan-Yu, Yi-Shun Wang, and Yong Ni Lee. "Investigating Factors Affecting Learning Satisfaction and Perceived Learning in Flipped Classrooms: The Mediating Effect of Interaction." *Interactive Learning Environments* (2022): 1–22. https://doi.org/10.1080/10494820.2021.2018616.

Matusiak, Krystyna K., Chelsea Heinbach, Anna Harper, and Michael Bovee. "Visual Literacy in Practice: Use of Images in Students' Academic Work." *College & Research Libraries* 80, no. 1 (2019): 123–139.

McDowell, Travis R., Emmalou T. Schmittzehe, Amanda J. Duerden, Dan Cernusca, Harvest Collier, and Klaus Woelk. "A Student-Choice Model to Address Diverse Needs and Promote Active Learning." *Journal of Science Education and Technology* 28 (2019): 321–328.

Means, Barbara and Julie Neisler. "Teaching and Learning in the Time of COVID: The Student Perspective." *Online Learning* 25, no. 1 (2021): 8–27.

O'Connor, Kate. "Constructivism, Curriculum and the Knowledge Question: Tensions and Challenges for Higher Education." *Studies in Higher Education* 47, no. 2 (2022): 412–422.

Persohn, Lindsay. "Curation as Methodology." *Qualitative Research* 21, no. 1 (2021): 20–41.

Raković, Mladen, Zahia Marzouk, Amna Liaqat, Philip H. Winne, and John C. Nesbit. "Fine Grained Analysis of Students' Online Discussion Posts." *Computers & Education* 157 (2020): 103982. https://doi.org/10.1016/j.compedu.2020.103982.

Schneider, Sascha. "Are There Never Too Many Choice Options? The Effect of Increasing the Number of Choice Options on Learning with Digital Media." *Human Behavior and Emerging Technologies* 3, no. 5 (2021): 759–775.

Son, Eun Hye and Tara Penry. "Variations in Project-Based Course Design." *Journal of Problem Based Learning in Higher Education* (2022): 1–16. https://journals.aau.dk/index.php/pbl/article/view/6821.

Starr-Glass, David. "Purposefully-Designed and Mindfully-Facilitated Online Courses." In *Handbook of Research on Managing and Designing Online Courses in Synchronous and Asynchronous Environments*, edited by Gurhan Durak and Serkan Cankaya, 251–272. (Hershey, PA: IGI Global, 2021).

Swan, Glenda. "Minorities' Views and Minorities Viewed: Embracing Minorities in the Classroom and Visual Culture." In *Fostering a Climate of Inclusion in the College Classroom: The Missing Voice of the Humanities* edited by Lavonna Lovern, 73–90. (Cham, Switzerland: Springer, 2018).

Vasodavan, Vinothini, Dorothy DeWitt, Norlidah Alias, and Mariani Md Noh. "E-moderation Skills in Discussion Forums: Patterns of Online Interactions for Knowledge Construction." *Pertanika Journal of Social Sciences and Humanities* 28, no. 4 (2020): 3025–3045.

CHAPTER 6

Conclusion

This book is based in my discipline-specific training and multiple decades of classroom experience, but it is written with the goal of sharing my knowledge in the same way I do as a teacher: with observations, suggestions, resources, and examples, but without being overly prescriptive. While this can be challenging for students—who are so often focused on finding the single correct answer—I trust that this somewhat more flexible approach to knowledge will be welcomed by fellow educators, as academia draws those attracted to challenge, investigation, and discovery. For example, despite the fact that images are a central focus of this book, I decided not to include any actual depictions in this book. I find that seeing a specific image can sometimes make it more difficult to visualize another image in its place, and I very much wanted to make this text more akin to a "create your own adventure," where the readers decide what path they want to follow, selecting images that are appropriate for their own content and courses.

This is also something that relates to students, as there is no single narrative that determines students' path to their chosen degree. Nevertheless, more students are coming into higher education with the expectation that their course-work focus will be on professional, post-graduate career skills, which also connected with how many institutions are marketing themselves.[1] While there certainly are a number of professional preparation courses—general as well as discipline-specific—most higher education courses are focused on teaching transferable skills which students will need to be able adapt to meet the various skills and roles required by their employment.[2] This makes it all the more important that courses focused on non-contemporary content establish their relevancy to the future and explain to students the flexibility of the skills associated with their study. I have no doubt that the way forward can come from the

[1] Bunce (2019).
[2] Fettes et al. (2020).

© The Author(s), under exclusive license to Springer Nature
Switzerland AG 2023
G. Swan, *ReEnvisioning the Material Past*,
https://doi.org/10.1007/978-3-031-24027-0_6

past, because learning comes from the process of understanding, analyzing, and evaluating. After all, material culture has been an aspect of human life at every stage of its development, and it continues even in today's digital world.[3]

Understandably, though, students will need assistance, support, and mentoring as they forge their own—sometimes winding—path to learning. Indeed, a large part of our role as instructors needs to focus on helping students understand the process and complexity of effective learning. While instructors may understand how important it is to progress from concrete to abstract knowledge and support that learning with self-analysis of the effectiveness of their learning strategies, this is rarely something students understand or undertake without prompting. For this reason, it is critical that instructors integrate the theory behind the process of learning into the course design.[4] Start by explaining to students how there are hierarchical levels of thinking and learning, as well as how specific aspects of an activity or a series of sequential activities were specifically designed by the instructor to help them progress from lower to higher orders of thinking. Of course, it helps to translate this into language students can easily understand; for example, I often employ the simile of constructing staircases in a building where activities and ideas get more complicated on each floor. As students slowly work their way to the top, help make the process as engaging as possible by providing choice, noting how skills and ideas might transfer, and how concepts might relate it to something in their own experience.

While it is always enjoyable to complement students when they have added a tool to their construction tool kit after building some stairs, plan on sharing both passive and active support at every significant step in this challenging but rewarding process. A course's learning management system makes it easy to share checklists, tips, support materials, and online resources in addition to the more common posting of instructions and rubrics. While many of these materials can be prepared and posted in advance, some should be responsive to what students are expressing or submitting; for example, if several students appear to be encountering a similar difficulty in a class discussion or submission, specifically announce to the class that support material has been added to expand or assist in a particular skill or topic related to that course content or activity. Incorporating student elements of self-assessment and reflection in association with course activities not only foster students' awareness of their own learning—which is referred to as metacognition[5]—but also provides invaluable information for the instructor.

However, be aware that students will need help in how to accurately self-assess. Students will often believe they understand course content when they do not.[6] Many students are become accustomed to a "one and done" way of

---

[3] Mardon and Belk (2018).
[4] Callaghan-Koru and Aqil (2022).
[5] Stanton et al. (2021).
[6] Avhustiuk (2020).

thinking about course activities and don't allow enough time for preparation or review. As a corollary, student will sometimes avoid examining their own mistakes with the goal of identifying future improvements. For all these reasons, it is important to be prepared to reframe and redirect frustration. I have found it useful to explain to students how encountering a roadblock can be useful because it helps them to find their own way to a solution, and I will freely share examples of my own failures that eventually transformed into valuable knowledge. To help students to retraining their own approach to learning, incorporate scaffolded elements within or across course activities along with moments for self-assessment, reflection, and feedback—by the instructor or peers. Consider asking students to self-identify a skill that needs further development, a difficulty discovered within an activity, or a question for further research, then have each student specifically target that issue as part of a future activity. Of course, don't forget to celebrate small, hard-won victories of any type with individual students, as positive reflection on one's improvement is some of the best encouragement of all. All this type of student support—both academic and emotional—has been demonstrated to increase students' satisfaction in their education.[7]

Encouraging student reflection about their performance on course content is also useful for generating more meaningful feedback on student evaluations of instruction. Many of those evaluation questions focus on issues about how the class was organized, the effectiveness of instructor feedback, and student learning; students who have become accustomed to being metacognitive about their own learning are able to provide much more direct and specific reflection rather than responding more emotionally in regard to what they did and did not like about the course. For example, as I discussed earlier, one semester there were a large number of students in my Mythology in World art course who really struggled with preparing effective notecards. However, in the student evaluations at the end of that course, there were still a significant number of students who cited that specific activity in response to the question that asked, "What did the instructor do that most helped your learning?" One student even remarked, "Even though it was tedious trying to keep up with the notecards every week, they really helped with understanding how to study for the tests." For me, I was really excited by this comment, as it showed how the student had reflected and been able to distinguish between a lack of personal enjoyment in this weekly activity and the beneficial learning that came from it.

Of course, educators also benefit from self-reflection about their own pedagogical choices in terms of both design and execution in association with student success in a course. Indeed, identifying and working on pedagogical improvements is often required by many institutions and can be important for evidence of a faculty member's professional development. Increasing student awareness and effectiveness in working with material culture—which this book documents is a skill that is both critical and underdeveloped—is something that

---

[7] Geier (2021).

would make a relevant, focused, and documentable goal for any faculty member. Below is an outline of how one might approach setting a small goal focused on helping students to improve their visual literacy in association with course content:

- Plan a single course activity that asks the students to engage with an image of material culture. Some possible examples include:

  - Explaining how elements of the style, content, and function of a particular image provides insight into the time period and culture in which it was made; consider requiring students to cite assigned course documents to support their points.
  - Comparing and contrasting an image to a related textual passage, citing both visual and textual evidence in support of their points.
  - Finding an image to accompany an assigned textual passage—or even an already existing essay by the student—explaining what aspects of the style, content, and function of the image provide a useful comparison or contrast to the text.

- Establish clear and measurable goals for at least three levels of performance.
- Design a rubric for the activity that can be shared with students as well as used in the reporting of results.
- Incorporate a couple of examples into class that demonstrate how the analysis of images in connection with the typically presented course content to support this new activity.
- Post an expanded version of at least one of these presented examples on the class learning management system in a format where it could be accessed by students and utilized as a supporting resource for the new activity.
- Collect a reflection from students on what they learned from the experience of working with material culture rather than simply relying on text alone. In addition to making a required element within the activity, consider adding a question on the student evaluations at the end of the semester if that is something permitted by your institution.
- Consider using the activity as part of a formal pre- and post-activity assessment. Show the image before the relevant content unit is presented in the course—or even as early as the first or second course meeting—to gather student responses as well as generate interest in upcoming content. Then, after the relevant content unit is presented, formally require the activity, but be sure to add a required reflection by students on how and why their own responses differed from the image's first presentation.

If your goals for incorporating more material culture into your course are much larger in scale, look into your institution's support of course improvement so that you might secure funding for professional development or even other type of compensation. Also, be sure to explore how the goal of helping students to improve their visual literacy in association with course content might effectively relate to specific university initiatives associated with the promotion of issues such as student engagement, retention, or mentoring. For example, undergraduate research is strongly correlated with student engagement and retention,[8] and the visual presentation of research content along with appropriate images is a natural component of research posters presented at academic conferences; so, consider a research assignment that requires students to present their poster to the rest of the class and then encourage the students with the most effective posters to present at a local or regional undergraduate research symposium and serve as a mentor for that process.

Ultimately, though, I hope this book has helped to make the idea of working with images—and making more connections with students through them—more approachable. Perhaps the reader will find comfort from the following admission: the speed with which images have become such a ubiquitous part of our everyday communication is something that even someone who holds an advanced degree focused on the analysis of images finds surprising and, at times, overwhelming. If so, even more comfort will come from the fact when I first shared this feeling with some students, they said they even they sometimes felt the same way! Now, though, I have become accustomed asking these "digital natives" to educate me in online resources or apps to help us all relate something old to something new. Indeed, many students seem very excited about the notion about contributing to our class, even sometimes even reaching out to me with a link long after our class has ended. I will allow this example to serve as my final reminder about the multiplicity of ways that instructors can employ visual communication with their students.

REFERENCES

Ambos, Elizabeth L. "Undergraduate Research in the United States: Diversity, Growth, and Challenges." In *International Perspectives on Undergraduate Research*, edited by Nancy H. Hensel and Patrick Blessinger, 19–38. (Cham, Switzerland: Palgrave Macmillan, 2020).

Avhustiuk, Maria. "Metacognitive Monitoring Accuracy and Learning Achievement Success of University Students." *Psychological Prospects Journal* 36 (2020): 10–21.

Bunce, Louise. "The Voice of the Student as a 'Consumer.'" In *Engaging Student Voices in Higher Education*, edited by Simon Lygo-Baker Ian M. Kinchin, and Naomi E. Winstone, 55–70. (Cham, Switzerland: Palgrave Macmillan, 2019).

Callaghan-Koru, Jennifer A., and Anushka R. Aqil. "Theory-Informed Course Design: Applications of Bloom's Taxonomy in Undergraduate Public Health Courses." *Pedagogy in Health Promotion* 8, no. 1 (March 2022): 75–83.

---

[8] Ambos (2020).

Fettes, Trisha, Karen Evans, and Elnaz Kashefpakdel. "Putting Skills to Work: It's Not So Much the What, or Even the Why, But How…." *Journal of Education and Work* 33, no. 2 (2020): 184–196.

Geier, Michael T. "Students' Expectations and Students' Satisfaction: The Mediating Role of Excellent Teacher Behaviors." *Teaching of Psychology* 48, no. 1 (2021): 9–17.

Mardon, Rebecca, and Russell Belk. "Materializing Digital Collecting: An Extended View of Digital Materiality." *Marketing Theory* 18, no. 4 (2018): 543–570.

Stanton, Julie Dangremond, Amanda J. Sebesta, and John Dunlosky. "Fostering Metacognition to Support Student Learning and Performance." *CBE—Life Sciences Education* 20, no. 2 (2021): 1–7. https://doi.org/10.1187/cbe.20-12-0289.

Index

© The Author(s), under exclusive license to Springer Nature
Switzerland AG 2023
G. Swan, *ReEnvisioning the Material Past*,
https://doi.org/10.1007/978-3-031-24027-0

Printed by Printforce, the Netherlands